MELLOW YOUR MONEY

alsace.loraine.publishing@gmail.com

ISBN: 979-8-9874561-0-1 (paperback)
ISBN: 979-8-9874561-1-8 (ebook)
ISBN: 979-8-9874561-2-5 (hardcover)
ISBN: 979-8-9874561-3-2 (audiobook)

Ordering Information:
Special discounts are available on quantity purchases by corporations, associations, and others. For details, contact alsace.loraine.publishing@gmail.com

MELLOW YOUR
MONEY

HOW TO SURF THE MARKET AND BUILD WEALTH WITHOUT STRESSING YOURSELF OUT

MICK HEYMAN

I dedicate this book to Dr. Terry Schwartz, who taught me that not only our challenges, but our foibles, missteps, and even those most disagreeable people are all gifts. They are our greatest teachers and, importantly, most of them can give us a good laugh—often at ourselves.

ACKNOWLEDGMENTS

To my kids, Vince, Alexander, and Sophie, who have heard most of these stories many times and encouraged me to write them down, though I suspect their motivation might be that they think that having written them, they won't have to listen to them again. We'll see about that.

To my dad, whose love and support helped give me the strength to overcome so many of my greatest challenges. He also showed me how to love a career and to appreciate the wonderful people that accompany us along the way. We've shared many special moments—and lost a few too many Bengals games—but I feel very lucky we've done so much together.

To my mom, who I miss so much and who touched me and all around her with love, inspiration, and infectious laughter. She never judged me no matter what I fessed up to. It meant so much that I could tell her anything, though she might get a little picky about my grammar!

To my wonderful editor, Beverly West, who helped me to relive these stories and uncover their color, depth, and humor. It has been such a fun path, not only to share our stories but to delve into the lessons at the foundation of so many of my misadventures. Her ability to help bring my writing to life is a brilliant talent.

To my sisters and their husbands, such a special family. We've always been there for each other and thankfully never judge ourselves too harshly! They are an amazing support and a lot of fun too!

To so many of my teachers but particularly Noel Vaughn, who helped teach me the fun of writing.

To Bill Sena, who gave me a start along this path of investing and showed me it's okay to be a little eccentric along the way.

To my friends and coworkers through the years, especially Carl Hafele and Jeff Krumpelman. We enjoyed much success and some bungles along the way too, but they taught me so much and certainly made the journey enjoyable.

To Dr. Jeff Baker, who kept me healthy in mind, body, and spirit with his remedies as well as his words of wisdom.

To Mr. Stroud, who has long passed but I wish I could have thanked personally for helping me long ago to learn to speak and express myself.

To Trudy Wheeler, who cautioned me to never be an actor and said I would be just fine being myself.

To the many authors who have inspired me with wisdom and/or humor through the years: Edwin Lefèvre (Jesse Livermore), Fyodor Dostoevsky, Jim Murray, Hal McCoy, Christopher Moore, Tom Robbins, Dale Carnegie, Stuart Wilde, Timothy Gallwey, Allan Watts, Sun Bear, and Tim Dorsey.

To the many that helped me at Book Launchers: You all were great and I appreciate all your help and handholding!

CONTENTS

INTRODUCTION

Mellow Money = Mellow Life

My first boss, Ken, was famous for his pregnant pauses. I assumed that sometimes these were designed to give him time to think, to formulate a measured response, to wait out the emotion of the moment, but other times I think he was just taking a break. It was my first week on the job and I found myself in the middle of one of these infamous pauses after completing my first assignment for the firm. He had asked me to write up an analysis of some stocks we had just purchased for our clients. He had read through my report and now I was in his office, awaiting his verdict.

Ken closed his eyes and rested his chin on his palm. Then, he began to shake his head back and forth, as if something was really bothering him. He frowned. And he kept on frowning as the clock ticked the minutes away. I just sat there, frozen, and vaguely terrified. Suddenly, he broke the stillness, seemed to be about to say something, but in the end, merely resumed his frowning. Finally, he sighed and looked straight into my eyes. Then he ripped up my work and threw it in the trashcan.

"Do you think our clients are idiots?" he boomed as my mouth went dry.

"Your first sentence here states that AT&T is the largest phone company in America. What moron doesn't know that, except maybe you?!" In hindsight it was an awfully stupid thing to write, especially considering that this was 1980 and AT&T was essentially the *only* phone company in America. But there were literally hundreds of methods he could have chosen to teach me that lesson. He chose a way that humiliated me and would stick in my memory for over 40 years.

This was the beginning of my relationship with Ken's extraordinary pauses. Every time I had a new stock pick or an idea about where the market was going, I would be greeted with Ken's ponderous ellipses. His chin would sink into his hand, his head would shake slowly back and forth, his eyes would close, and then that frown would appear. What would happen when the pause ended? Would it be a smile, laughter, agreement, or ridicule? It was anybody's guess.

It would take a few years—and a little therapy—but eventually I began to realize that these were learning opportunities for me. A chance to begin to grow up and deal with insecurities that had been with me for most of my life. These terrifying moments were actually stepping stones in my development. After all, if I could experience adversity and even ridicule and overcome them, I could then be brave enough to take risks in an uncertain environment where each stock purchase was always a chance for disaster. It took practice, but then one day I was prepared. I'd given Ken yet another one of my stock analyses and was once again confronted with the mighty pause and frown. Finally, I'd had enough. I dug down deep inside myself, and I found my voice.

"Ken, you probably don't realize this, but these long pauses and the insults that follow really make me feel bad. They undermine my self-worth, and they certainly aren't helping me come up with any new ideas." When I'd said my piece, I paused, for a change, and Ken looked at me a little startled. I held his gaze. I refused to look away. I waited out the silence for the first time without fear. I stood my ground and held my position. I started thinking about where I might find my second job. I realized I had options. Then, finally, Ken smiled and nodded his head yes instead of shaking it no. "Yes, Mick," he said, "I can see that you're right."

I felt such freedom and exhilaration after this victory. And it opened my eyes to many things. I had learned what Ken had consciously, or more likely unconsciously, been teaching me all along about how to deal with the demons of disapproval, how to take risks and face the consequences—even the humiliating ones. How to overcome disastrous choices by learning from them, and how to grow as a human being, and as an analyst.

These are just a few of the lessons that we need to learn in order to lean back and enjoy success, without fear. The only true security is confidence in our ability to take a pause, form a measured judgment, and then stand our ground, face the consequences good or bad, and grow from every experience, both in the market, and in our lives. How thankful I am to Ken for waking me up to the importance of understanding my feelings and then expressing them in a constructive way. Learning to deal with fear and uncertainty is what living a good life, and being a good investor, is all about. Ken gave me the best possible launch pad into a world that can plummet or soar in a heartbeat and defy even the best logic of the experts.

As in the market, so it goes in life.

Much like golf, the market is a metaphor for just about everything. Emotion and psychology move markets. Human perception impacts economies and influences how we assess world events—and our portfolios.

The markets will unmask both our greatest weaknesses and reveal our greatest strengths. If we have the humility to admit mistakes, and as Jesse Livermore, the great trader back in the early 1900s suggested, use our mistakes as a "tuition fee," so much personal growth will result, which will, in turn, ease the quality of our lives and mellow our money.

I have decided to share my knowledge about the market through the stories that shaped me and my investment philosophy. I believe that the best lessons are the ones we learn the hard way, through human connection, and in the trenches of experience. Though I majored in economics, my favorite courses were in Russian literature: I loved the emotion, the power of the stories, and the study of human nature—as you will see from the anecdotes in this book, it's my long-held interest in literature, psychology, and philosophy that have helped me understand the market in a uniquely human way. By sharing my stories and the lessons they taught me, it is my hope that you can both benefit from my experience and come to see your own stories, good and bad, as great teaching moments in your life. Though we all have different paths, the emotional highs and lows they produce are common to us all.

I would like readers to come away with the understanding that money is just another expression of us, what we value, what our goals are, how we handle triumph and defeat, how we stumble—and get back up—and what mark we want to leave on the world. After a lifetime of riding the market highs and lows, I have discovered that when we find greater balance in our finances, it leads to greater balance in our lives, and vice versa.

These are the stories that made a big impression on me and have embedded themselves in my investment philosophy. They are the moments and relationships that have helped me to become who I am, both as a person and as an advisor. There have been challenges and victories and plenty of defeats, but every time there were invaluable lessons to learn. We all struggle with difficult emotions at times, and we will all confront psychological challenges. How we deal with them informs how we grow as individuals and how we become enriched as investors.

I hope that reading this book is a fun and worthwhile adventure for you. And if you ever need help in learning how to take a long pause, just let me know, as I had the best teacher in the world. I too am now adept at taking a beat, gathering my thoughts, and mellowing the ride.

HOW DO YOU SOLVE A PROBLEM LIKE ELOISE?

The Theory of Benign Neglect

When I graduated from college and took my very first job, I imagined myself learning from the kings of Wall Street about the masterful moves that unlocked the doors of market dominance. I saw all sorts of shiny objects on the path ahead: the excitement of huge windfalls, the thrill of making my clients rich beyond their wildest dreams. And there I would be, demonstrating my startling market insight—becoming so famous that Louis Rukeyser[1] of *Wall Street Week* would be begging me to join him on his show to share my secrets of investment wizardry.

Of course, one of the things I've learned after a lifetime in finance is that nothing ever turns out like you expect it will at the beginning, and that was certainly true for me, right from the get-go. Because one of my first mentors in the business was not a titan of industry or a Silicon Valley serial entrepreneur, but an ex-high school teacher named Eloise, who lived in a retirement home in Cincinnati.

When I look back on it now, I realize that it made total sense that my career would start out this way. My investment training had been unorthodox, to put it mildly. My least favorite subject in college was economics, though it was my major. I learned statistics from a professor who explained the subject to me by calculating my low odds of passing his course, right before advising me to drop the class. Much to the professor's astonishment, however, I did finally pass statistics, although it took a few tries.

My favorite subjects were philosophy, psychology, and literature, particularly Russian literature with its tortured portraits of people skirting the edge and coming back wiser, and often more at peace. I didn't understand back then that Dostoevsky was way better preparation for a career on Wall Street than a statistics class would ever be. Sound investment strategy requires that you understand what the numbers are telling you, certainly, but it also requires you to listen carefully to what is underlying the gyrations in the market.

Whether I am investing in a particular stock or the market as a whole, I want to know the story of what is behind the movement in prices. What are the current challenges, worries, or obstacles? Why the potential optimism or pessimism from investors? Why so extreme? What does the recent history of stock performance tell me about the future? Not that earnings and sales and interest rates are unimportant but how they got to where they are is just as important, as well as weighing the odds of the future direction. I didn't know it then, but studying economics turned out to be all about interpreting human behavior.

If you listen, money will tell you a story

My relationship with my client, Eloise, began in the back seat of an Oldsmobile Cutlass Supreme. "Young man," she said to me as my boss introduced us on that first day, "we want to find a car that is big enough to fit three fat old ladies in the back seat." Eloise said this without a hint of irony or embarrassment. She was merely acquainting me with the facts as she saw them, because for some reason she thought I needed to know them.

I just stood there with a sheepish grin on my face. I don't think I said anything. I tried to respond but came up short. Nobody had warned me that my first task as an associate was going to be helping an old woman buy a car. It sounds benign on the surface, but in the moment, I was inexplicably terrified. I realized, suddenly, that I knew almost nothing about buying cars, and even less about old women. The little that I had just witnessed, however, made me think that Eloise would do a way better job negotiating the deal than I ever could. I also had a feeling that Eloise knew that as well as I did.

"Mick here is going to come with you today and help you find the perfect car, and he'll find it at the perfect price too, isn't that right, Mick?" my boss said, smiling, pretending not to notice that his young associate had turned bright red. "You take Miss Eloise on over to the Oldsmobile dealership now and ask for my friend Dan. Tell him I sent you. He'll take real good care of you."

I was already familiar with my boss Ken's holistic approach to client service. It was one of the things that attracted me to the firm. Ken was a people person, and his firm put client experience at the top of their priority list. Now I was learning what that meant firsthand. It meant listening to your client, adjusting your services to match their needs, and caring enough to know when and how to fulfill their expectations. It also apparently meant helping Eloise shop for a new car with a generous back seat and finding it at a discount to boot.

After another long and uncomfortable silence, Eloise and I, along with her eclectic entourage, piled into the car and headed for the nearest dealership. Eloise was right, she needed a bigger vehicle—the woman never traveled alone. In addition to myself, there was her retired maid, Alma, her retired cook, Frieda, and her "chauffer," Jimmy Lee, who was truly terrifying behind the wheel, but who, Eloise informed me, was an excellent tap dancer. Jimmy Lee and I got off to a slow start because he wanted Eloise to buy a Cadillac. Ken's friend Dan and the Oldsmobile dealership idea did not go down well with him at all.

"There is no way no Oldsmobile ever gonna run like a Cadillac, Mick," he said, looking at me instead of the road. "Probably isn't as safe nor as comfortable as a Cadillac neither. Or as quiet or pretty, that's for sure."

I stammered out something about costs and benefits, which sounded flat and unconvincing next to Jimmy Lee's glowing superlatives. Thankfully, Eloise stepped in to rescue me.

"Jimmy, you drive us on over to the Oldsmobile dealership right now," she commanded, sounding like she had been issuing orders like this all of her life. I realize she probably had.

"Yes, Miss Eloise," said Jimmy Lee, who knew which side his bread was buttered. I looked back at Eloise, who smiled at me and winked. I knew with that wink that she liked me, and to my surprise, I was starting to like her back.

After some fairly anemic negotiating on my part, and a much more effective call between Dan and my boss, we got the deal done and drove off the lot with a brand-new powder blue Oldsmobile Ninety-Eight, complete with the world's most enormous back seat. That experience bonded Eloise and me. I had delivered, and as far as she was concerned, that made us instant friends. I also think she saw in me someone who knew very little but cared a lot, and somebody who genuinely wanted to help. She was right about that. I do like to help. At the end of that day, Eloise invited me to dinner the following Monday at her retirement home, and so began a weekly date that I came to enjoy as much as I hope Eloise did.

It did take me a while to adjust to her style. Eloise was a larger-than-life woman with a larger-than-life personality, and a voice to match. She made liberal use of all of these attributes, often in otherwise quiet situations. The minister of her church told me about his first experience with Eloise. He was delivering his first sermon to the congregation when, 10 minutes into the sermon, Eloise bellowed from her first-row seat, "Pastor, we know it's your first day and you're trying real hard, but could you move it along?"

Whatever jumped out of Eloise's mouth was exactly how she felt at the time, no guardrails. Eloise was full of life, a complete eccentric, taking charge of every moment, and seemingly immune to embarrassment. After passing gas, she would look up with satisfaction and a big smile and say, "Wow! That felt good!"

Yet somehow, Eloise never crossed the line and became outright rude. No question she marched right up to it, but she never strayed so far into uncouth territory that people held it against her. Like a character in a 19th-century novel, Eloise was a study in contradictions. She was at once demure and blunt, canny and vulnerable, privileged and crass. In other words, she was quintessential Dostoevsky, and so it was no wonder I was drawn to her mystery.

Caring is the coin of the realm

My weekly date with Eloise invariably began by eating dinner with her, Alma, and Frieda in the dining room of her retirement home. She would introduce me to her many friends as "the gentleman who handles my money and helps me give it away." After a mushy beige dinner that always tasted the same no matter what I ordered, we would head up to Eloise's room to take care of our weekly business.

The four of us would wander slowly down the long hallway toward the elevator, which toiled and groaned its way up to Eloise's suite on the fifth floor. As a young man, I felt years of my life melting into the acoustic tile. It took centuries to ride that elevator up. Finally, the doors would shudder and open, Frieda and Alma would head left, and we would head right.

Eloise had two rooms—her bedroom and the living room, which was dominated by a card table right in the middle, piled a foot high with hundreds of requests from various charities, all hungry for a check. Eloise had $2,000 a month set aside for charitable giving, and she took this quite seriously as she weighed the requests.

Ken later explained to me that Eloise came from a prominent Cincinnati family who had contributed generous gifts of money and time in the city for generations. Eloise was genuine, Gilded Age, minted Cincinnati royalty. Her father had been the medical director of the Cincinnati Tuberculosis Sanatorium for over 40 years and never took a salary. He worked unpaid in what, back then, they called a "pest house," treating incurably ill and contagious patients for free in order to advance medical science in the war on TB. When he retired, the hospital was renamed for him in appreciation of his years of unpaid service, not to mention his generous financial gifts to the hospital.

After a brief stint working with Orson Welles[2], Eloise's only brother died in World War II. Eloise never married. She worked as a teacher in the Cincinnati public school system until she retired. She, like her father, never accepted a salary. Three generations of service and philanthropy had trickled down to Eloise. Now that legacy was in my care.

Every week we would sit down to her mountain of requests. And every week we would go through the pile and select the lucky recipients. I can still remember Eloise's thoughtful pauses as I read out each charity name. Then, when we hit the right one, she would joyfully shout out, "Young man, let's give $133.76 to the symphony!" or "$93.54 to the Lakota Sioux!"

We could only complete a handful of envelopes each week. And I knew that even if I came every week from now until I was as old as Eloise, we never would have made our way through that pile. Every time she headed to the bathroom I would dump as many as I could in the trash. Invariably though, when I returned the following week, the pile was just as high or even higher.

Eloise

TEACHERS YOU CAN TAKE TO THE BANK

Dead Poets Society (1989)[3]

DIRECTOR: *Peter Weir*

STARS: *Robin Williams, Robert Sean Leonard, Ethan Hawke*

This Robin Williams classic about a maverick teacher who inspires his students to seize the day through classic poetry reminds us of the power we can unlock when we connect dusty old theories from the past to the emotions and experiences of the present.

Stand and Deliver (1988)[4]

DIRECTOR: *Ramón Menéndez*

STARS: *Edward James Olmos, Estelle Harris*

The true story of high school teacher, James Escalante, who inspires his at-risk students, whom everyone expects to drop out, to master calculus. This school of hard knocks classic shows us what we miss when we judge a book by its cover.

School of Rock (2003)[5]
DIRECTOR: *Richard Linklater*
STARS: *Jack Black, Mike White, Joan Cusack*
The infectious laughter and aspirational creativity of Jack Black is a refreshing lesson in how you have to break a few rules if you want to find the music.

Eventually, my check-writing duties diversified, and I began reading to Eloise during my visits. She was a member of several book clubs and so we began making our way through a pile of books in addition to the pile of donation requests. Our first book covered how the Panama Canal was built, which taught me more than I ever wanted to know about that particular subject. After each "work" session, Eloise insisted on writing me a check for $12.50 to compensate me for my time. I tried every time to turn it down, but she never let me. So, every Tuesday I would turn my check into the firm's bookkeeper and let her figure out how to account for it.

As a relatively shy recent college graduate, I must confess that Eloise was a handful for me. I came to understand, though, that as whacky as she might have seemed at times, people loved her, people remembered her, and people forgave her because in some way, big or small, she made their lives better. Eloise made a difference to people and that taught me that maybe I could emerge from my shell, become the character that I was meant to be, and in my own way, also make a difference. I regard this intensely human lesson as one of the most important in my portfolio—financial advisors need to understand how to put their clients' needs ahead of their own. Eloise taught me how to do that without cramping my style.

As my boss had learned long before I came along, the client comes first. The mantra was the cornerstone of the firm. This meant understanding your client's objectives and focusing on meeting those goals, rather than on your own expectations for their portfolio. I now know that this is rule number one of good management. For Eloise, it wasn't the return that was important, but rather her ability to have just enough money left over each month to give to others.

Eloise never knew the value of her portfolio and she didn't care. In fact, I was glad she didn't know because I never wanted Jimmy Lee to find out what she was worth, lest she wind up with a garage full of Cadillacs. What mattered to her was that she had that $2,000 a month after expenses to dole out in her own fashion, and in this way, stay true and connected to her family's legacy, to her church, and to her community.

The priority for Eloise's portfolio as far as we were concerned was generating consistent, predictable income. Her account had to reliably produce enough income to cover her, Frieda, Alma, and Jimmy's costs, her weekly outings with her friends, and the $2,000 a month in charitable donations. This required what we jokingly called our plan of "benign neglect," which meant that when it came to Eloise's money, we did as little as was humanly possible.

Sometimes it's not what you do, but what you don't do that counts

Back in the 1980s, you might have expected us to invest Eloise's account heavily in money market funds and bonds that were paying high rates of interest and divesting her of her stocks. Her account, though, was formed in the thirties and forties when the philosophy of the firm was to buy high-quality common stocks that would continue to increase dividends over time. By the 1980s, these stocks were up over tenfold in some cases and continuing to raise dividends. And since capital gains rates were so high, it would have been crazy to sell quality stocks, pay taxes, and invest in bonds or money market funds. So, at over 80 years old, Eloise was nearly fully invested in stocks!

You might be thinking, that's insane! Why would you ever allow for this kind of potential volatility in an older person's portfolio? Well, the answer lies in the objective itself. Eloise simply cared about her monthly income and as long as we were providing what she needed in that regard, we were meeting her objective. Plus, we were making sure her income continued to grow because the quality stocks she owned consistently raised their dividends. She had no fear of volatility because it didn't concern her.

And how did Eloise's account perform over the course of the remainder of her life? Well, like many investment firms, we moved in and out of the market and in and out of various stocks to achieve returns. Most of our clients, unlike Eloise, focused on total returns and were managed in a balanced fashion with a degree of market timing. Yet despite our efforts to pick timely stocks and anticipate market highs and lows, unbelievably, we rarely outperformed Eloise's account—ironically, doing nothing consistently outperformed doing something. With her portfolio we focused on holding her quality stocks and not bothering to be influenced by short-term gyrations in the market.

Of course, our policy of benign neglect never involved neglecting Eloise herself. How could anyone ever do that? Or want to? We watched over her by listening and paying attention to what mattered most to her.

The conclusion, which took me many years and thousands of trades to arrive at, is that sometimes you can try too hard, and you can do too much. It is so temping to try to improve on long-term investing and take advantage of the emotional highs and lows that every stock and market experiences. What we have to remember, though, is that by losing a position in a good long-term holding we risk not getting back in, and so quite often we risk losing the kind of gain that can only occur over many years. Procter & Gamble,[6] Johnson & Johnson,[7] McDonalds,[8] and Colgate,[9] for example, have all multiplied by profound integers over many years, and one would only have had to hold on to capture a phenomenal long-term gain.

Imagine selling Apple or Microsoft after the first time they doubled or tripled—you would have left behind a fortune when all you had to do was hold on! In other words, all you had to do was nothing.

The benign neglect strategy doesn't have to mean sit still and forget your portfolio, but rather let the good stocks run, pare back occasionally, and let the long-term trends in prices work to your advantage.

Words You Can Take to the Bank

THE POWER OF SITTING

After spending many years in Wall Street..., I want to tell you this: It was never my thinking that made the big money for me. It was always my sitting. Got that? My sitting tight! It is no trick at all to be right on the market. You always find lots of early bulls in bull markets and early bears in bear markets. I've known many men who were right at exactly the right time and began buying or selling stocks when prices were at the very level which should show the greatest profit. And their experience invariably matched mine—that is, they made no real money out of it. Those men who can both be right and sit tight are uncommon. I found it one of the hardest things to learn.[10]
— EDWIN LEFÈVRE, *Reminiscences of a Stock Operator*, 1923

Rivers know this: there is no hurry. We shall get there some day.[11]
—A. A MILNE, *House at Pooh Corner*

Doing nothing is sometimes one of the highest of the duties of man.[12]
—G.K. CHESTERTON

Benign Neglect by the Numbers:

1. **Don't try to do too much in your portfolio.** Let the long-term trends in stocks help while you sit back and don't get in the way.

2. **Focus on your objectives.** If volatility is a concern, then make sure you limit your stock exposure. If income is your focus,

make sure you maximize income and limit how much you need to worry about volatility.

3. **Don't be afraid to share your thoughts and feelings—as crazy as they may sound.** Enjoy the interesting characters around you, learn from them, and then become one of them.

4. **For an investor in training, spend a little time reading Dostoevsky, because you're going to need it.**

▌ POSTSCRIPT:

I visited Eloise when she was in the hospital and close to death. I sat with her, and I let her know how much she had taught me about life and about my business. I was able to thank her for being such a remarkable first client and for teaching me so much about life. "Young man," she responded, and smiled in a way that brought her back the way I remembered her. "Can you please do me a favor and hand me over that big jar of candy behind you?" I handed it to her and she opened it gleefully. She popped a butterscotch into her mouth, and then she looked at me, and she winked.

CHAPTER 2

HEADLINES AND BOTTOM LINES
The Surprising History of Money

My first several months as a real live professional money man were not comfortable ones and they seemed to go on forever. Nobody looked very happy to see me. I felt like a side order of spinach on a dessert buffet—everybody was basically waiting for the server to take me off the table because I was an obvious mistake. My personal stock valuation was, generously, still a question mark. Beyond helping to buy Eloise a car and racking up checks for twelve dollars and fifty cents every week, I hadn't contributed much. I still dwelled in the realm of the possible.

I felt my utter uselessness most intensely at the partners' meeting each week. I'd sit there as everyone reported their exciting new business, their clients' stunning progress, or tips from their current research. Everyone had an area of specialty. Everyone knew something

I didn't know. I felt invisible at these meetings: nobody ever looked my way; nobody spoke to me. And why should they? What were they going to ask, "Hey Mick, what's the update on Eloise's two grand a month contribution and how's the construction of the Panama Canal coming along?" Those were the days when mentorship meant throwing the kid into the water to see if he would swim. I was kicking in the water, but so far, I was no closer to shore. And I could feel the tide going out.

When in search of a calling, pick up the phone

One day a whole new world opened to me in the form of a new "portable" computer the office had purchased for reasons nobody understood. From the moment I unwrapped the thing, I was fascinated. The new Compaq was sleek and chic and ultra-cool, despite being about as portable as a couch. Nobody knew what to do with the damn thing, even me—although I sensed the infinite possibilities.

"What a waste!" my boss said disparagingly in a way that made it unclear whether he was referring to me or the computer. "Nothing more than an oversized gimmick," said another partner, like it was my fault. Despite the generally dismissive and even hostile attitude firm-wide about this newfangled acquisition, I knew that this was my ticket.

I devoted untold hours exploring this new and much maligned contraption. One day I was reading through one of the weekly strategy reports that we received from a major brokerage firm out of New York. We would typically read these reports to look for information that was relevant and then, based on this data, form our own strategy. That's when I thought, why shouldn't we do our own research? Then we could input our own data into a chart on the handy Compaq and make all those big city brokers redundant…

At the very next partners' meeting, I opened my mouth and spoke to the group for the very first time. "What if we did our own research instead of relying on Wall Street?" I said tentatively, trying to read the room. "Why do they know more than us? We can make our own charts on the new computer. I mean, wouldn't our clients be impressed if they saw that we were doing our own original research?"

I swear people looked at me like I had just swallowed a frog. But then they thought about it for a minute and one of the partners said, "Great idea, Mick, now you make it happen."

Thus began an interminable period in the library researching data that stretched back many years so it could all be inputted into our new Compaq. There was no such thing as the Internet back then, so I had to build out the old data sufficiently to allow us to compare the new market data within a historical context the old-fashioned way. I was giving our Compaq, and thus our firm, long vision. And so, starting back in the 1920s, I began constructing my research, poring through old volumes of *Barron's* and other papers late into the night and on the weekends while my friends were out having fun.

Words You Can Take to the Bank

THE VALUABLE LESSONS OF HISTORY

He who knows only his own generation remains always a child.[13]
—GEORGE NORLIN

The four most dangerous words in investing are, this time it's different.[14]
—SIR JOHN TEMPLETON

If you don't know history, then you don't know anything. You are a leaf that doesn't know it is part of a tree.[15]
—MICHAEL CRICHTON

As I pored over my project as though my professional life depended upon it, which it probably did, I became fascinated watching history unfold again in the headlines. **1500 Dead in Hawaii, Congress Votes War** shouted the *New York World Telegram* after Pearl Harbor. **Japs Butcher Americans** shrieked the *San Antonio Express*. Then I would look to see what happened in the market after these grim headlines. Obviously, people's lives changed instantly once the war began. The economy shifted, the headlines were depressing, and yet ironically, the market started going up. Hmm. What was that about?

As I read further, I was riveted, not by the numbers, but by the unfolding story of history, playing out through the canyons of Wall Street, rippling through the Main Streets of America in a never-ending tide that ebbed and flowed. This was the moment I fell in love with the stock market.

Now, finally, I had something to offer at the table. Quite often, whenever market predictions came up, there I was, piping up with my historical perspective, trying to add narrative and context to the market discussion. I was like an English professor in a room full of number guys, but I didn't care. Of course, people were a little startled by my storytelling at first, and my chart-making had slowed my other work to a crawl, but what I was learning was important, and even the partners were starting to listen.

In a nutshell, what I was beginning to understand is that the big, cat-aclysmic moments in history that scream at us from the headlines, the ones that predict doom and disaster and market collapse, are usually wrong. Pearl Harbor did not plunge us into a depression, and neither did Black Monday in 1987.

Investors Beware! was *Barron's* headline on March 30, 2020[16] while the country pitched into the height of the pandemic. Did it frighten me as an investment manager? Of course it did. How could it not? I worried along with everybody else that the market might collapse, that a vaccine would never be found, that I would run out of toilet paper. And yet none of that actually happened.

Should I stay or should I go?

It can be difficult to tell the difference between fact and fantasy when it comes to money. It's hard to separate our hopes and fears from what is unfolding in the real world. Bad things happen and the market usually bottoms out for a moment. People predict doom, and doom rarely manifests. What I saw in the archive of dramatic headlines from the Great Depression forward, even when people are expecting the worst, is that the worst generally never happens. The same is true when people are expecting the best. Happy days rarely last long, and up until now, neither has the sky fallen.

Whether it was Pearl Harbor, the Korean War, the Kennedy assassination, or COVID, both in good times and in bad, often the headlines each week would have you believe the world was on the edge of something horrific. But it never happened. When the headlines were at their bleakest, good times invariably rose from the ashes. And when the headlines cheered that smooth sailing lay ahead, a collapse inevitably followed.

The movement of the market is nuanced, so take a breath before reacting

The story of history and the market can't be expressed in a headline. You can't understand Dostoevsky by reading the chapter titles. Pearl Harbor gets bombed, war is declared, the markets tank. That's the story in the headlines, but the truth is much more nuanced. For example, the market was down only a little over 6% in the few days after Pearl Harbor.[17] That was probably because Pearl Harbor happened on top of three years of declining prices and a 17% drop after the fall of France. Pearl Harbor coincided with the end of the decline in prices due to the Great Depression.[18] The market then *began* a sustained rise, increasing 20% in 1942, 26% in 1943, and 20% in 1944. So basically, Pearl Harbor, as far as the market was concerned, was not catastrophic. But no one would have predicted this on that dark day in December 1941.

Legends suggest that King Solomon inscribed these wise words, "This too shall pass" on his ring,[19] and from my first years in the investment business, after hours spent tracing the story of the market backward, I have made this thought my North Star.

Change is the only constant, and during times of great change, good or bad, you must anchor yourself to the things that endure: confidence in country, confidence in yourself, confidence in the market's desire to grow, and confidence in humanity's ability to rebound.

This is a perspective that my mother shared with King Solomon.

My mother developed breast cancer in her early 30s and despite all her efforts to fight it, the cancer kept coming back, ultimately metastasizing to her bones. Although she was young, her prognosis was poor. Remission was thought to be out of the question. It was a terrible, tortuous time, and yet against all odds, my mom kept coming back. And 30 years later, she was still around, making the doctors eat their words. The doctors were wrong about my mom because they were only reading the headlines. They didn't understand that my mom was a survivor—no matter what the cancer screens said, she had no intention of giving in.

The longer story, the one that the headlines didn't capture, was that my mom started life as a sweet, gentle person, who wanted only to please everyone in her life. This was nice for us kids, but I'm not sure how nice it was for her. My mom sacrificed a lot, maybe too much. And yet she had a brilliant creative side that she expressed every day through her artwork. My mom was an oil painter and a clay sculptor, and she held on to this, no matter what else was happening in her world. Through a divorce from my dad and all her bouts of cancer, she clung to her love for art, and it helped sustain her. The artistic spirit must have skipped a generation because I missed out, but my daughter sure inherited it as well as my mom's fighting spirit.

My mom also had a sense of humor. She loved to laugh, especially at inappropriate moments. She was a little like Eloise that way. She had some famous moments laughing in temple. Something awkward would happen, something as simple as a group of older people bickering loudly about what page the rabbi was directing us to, and suddenly my mom's laughter rang out. Soon we were all laughing along with her. Well, at least I was.

Though my mom found joy in her children and in her artwork, she did not have a joyful marriage. My parents had married young and probably were not a good match from the beginning. Their relationship was no picnic for either one of them. The inability to find happiness together made home life difficult, and then my mom's cancer came back. Though my parents struggled to stay together for us kids, eventually, they divorced. My mom was devastated, which surprised me a little.

I think my mom was always prepared for her marriage to end, but when it finally did, it took her by surprise and threw her off her game. She became depressed and resentful that her fantasy of a successful marriage and ideal family life had fallen apart. Now she was a divorced woman fighting cancer. When I look back at that time I wonder, how would her headlines have read? "Cancer victim's life goes from bad to worse, and she calls it quits at last!" With all the difficulties she faced at that time, the *Daily News* would have passed her off as a goner. But in fact, my mother was on the verge of entering the happiest years of her life.

"I'm going to show those sons of bitches looking at me with pity that Mary Lou is just fine and will walk again very soon, and they should all just be quiet and mind their own damn business!" my mother would declare. "Fine, Doctor, whatever you say, but just so you know, I'm going to outlive you!" she would tell the doctors who had just given her six months to live. I could see in their faces that they didn't believe her. I could see they were asking themselves silently, *just who is this crazy, indomitable woman*? Yet unbelievably, she did outlive a few of them.

The will to survive moves markets against all odds

What the doctors and everyone including me came to understand is that my mom lived because she had a passion to live. And that's a hard concept to explain in a few words. After the divorce, my mom traveled the world. She dated; she broke up with beaus just because they no longer suited her. She sang at piano bars until the wee hours of the morning even though she could not carry a tune in a bucket. She once sang a Passover song so out of tune that it took us years to remember how the real tune went.

Most importantly, my mom fell in love again. She met Syd, who had recently lost his own wife to cancer. They were inseparable from the moment they met, and it was quickly evident to us all that they were made for each other. They spent the happiest years of my mom's life together, and Syd took care of my mom in her final days as if he had been by her side for 50 years.

My beautiful mom

THE HISTORY OF MONEY

The Great Gatsby (1974)[20]

DIRECTOR: *Jack Clayton*

STARS: *Robert Redford, Mia Farrow*

This lavish portrait of wealth, opulence, and decadence in the Roaring Twenties is a cautionary tale about the cost of wealth disparity, and a reminder of the dangers of feeling invulnerable to the inevitable ebb and flow of the market and of life. There is also a great remake with Leonardo DiCaprio.[21]

Seabiscuit (2003)[22]

DIRECTOR: *Gary Ross*

STARS: *Tobey Maguire, Jeff Bridges, Chris Cooper*

Not just a film of redemption for the owner, trainer, jockey, and even the horse, but a great portrayal of what Americans endured at the end of the twenties and throughout the Great Depression. It also illustrates that despite the struggle, life moves on and there will always be a next phase that can bring redemption.

Of Mice and Men (1992)[23]

DIRECTOR: *Gary Sinise*

STARS: *John Malkovich, Gary Sinise*

This story of two men who dream of owning land is a fascinating look into the endurance of the allure of the American Dream, even during the Dust Bowl of the Great Depression.

There is always another cookie

Toward the very end of her life, my mom traveled quite a distance to visit us. She did this, although it must have been an excruciating ride, because she wanted to meet my newborn son—her third grandchild—before she became too weak to hold him. By this time, she had been battling cancer for over 30 years. The cancer had spread to almost every organ in her body, including her brain. She had endured countless broken bones, and after each break, she had willed herself back to health. My mother refused to relent.

She and Syd arrived at our house on a Saturday afternoon. She looked ill and rushed immediately to the bathroom. Syd explained that she had felt ill from mile one. When she came back, she looked haggard and sat down at the kitchen table. When we handed over my son for her to hold, all the pain instantly left her face to be replaced by a sublime smile. She looked perfectly and completely happy, enjoying this moment that she had fought so hard to be present for. Then, after a few precious moments, she passed her grandson back to me and said, "That's it! That's all I wanted. I don't need anything else. I'm done."

A long silence fell over us all. Nobody spoke—we all knew what she meant. We empathized with what she had been through, and none was willing to encourage her to do anything more. We could not see another reason for her to fight on. All was accomplished. It was a moment of sadness, of appreciation for her courage, of acknowledgment that she had the right to call it quits and hopefully find peace at what appeared to be the end.

Then suddenly, my mom spied a plateful of freshly baked chocolate chip cookies sitting temptingly on the kitchen counter. "Well, that's it I guess," she said with a mischievous grin replacing the exhaustion on her face, "except for maybe one more cookie. Pass them over!" And then my mom laughed that infamous and inappropriate giggle of hers, and we all heaved a sigh of relief. We were once again united, and life could continue.

So, here's the thing I want us all to remember. Life goes on, and so does money—often against all odds, and in defiance of what the forecasters will tell you. Whether the market surges or plunges, it's never as good or as bad as they say in the headlines...and there is always the next cookie.

Lessons I Learned from the History of Money

- **Find balance in your approach to managing your life and your money.** We can become less affected by the whims and volatility of the market when we understand that everything changes back, and then changes again. We can set our objective and see how, over time, even with the inevitable ups and downs, we can eventually achieve our goals through balance, patience, and a grounding in the things that endure.

- **The next time there is some horrible news that the market panics over and things look bleak, search the Internet and read what was said at other bleak moments in history.** Take comfort that those who were living through it then were feeling what you're going through now and survived. In this way, we can find hope that "this too shall pass" and realize that everything old is new again, and vice versa.

- **Remember to laugh and to sing, to paint or sculpt, to do what you love, and put your faith in what endures.**

- **Stop being so serious!** Living is meant to be fun, and some degree of risk enhances the flavor of life.

CHAPTER 3

TIPPY CANOE AND A FISH STORY TOO

Real Risk Versus Perceived Risk

I must confess right here at the top: I am not a gifted outdoorsman. I did try camping as a teenager, around the time when young men are traditionally led out into the woods to pit themselves against the elements. The elements always won. Every single time. I was never sure if that's the whole point, but then I thought it was still a contest, and I was not making a good showing. My memories of these escapades are spotty and tortured; vague impressions of extreme discomfort: sweltering heat, damp sleeping bags, and bugs. Lots and lots of bugs.

There was one brief, shining moment of glory when I caught a fish while on a canoe trip, although to be fair, it was more like the fish caught me. I had fallen asleep in the canoe and woke up to calm waters, a gentle breeze, and a monster northern pike on the line. I started cranking my reel, trying to participate at least a little bit in my good fortune. My intervention felt redundant.

At one point, a counselor came paddling over, then seized the fish, pulled it up out of the water with his bare hands, and threw it into my boat. Later, he filleted the fish with his buck knife and cooked it for us all over a roaring campfire. It turned out to be the biggest catch that summer. In the blink of an eye, I was a fishing god.

Ironically, it was during this same trip that I had another outdoor experience that stuck with me into my adult life. In all the excitement after my accidental encounter with the great fish, I let myself be talked into taking a midnight canoe trip. One of the counselors had asked us to check on the canoes and make sure we had brought them all far enough onto shore that afternoon. Apparently, the current had a curious way of creeping up onto the banks and stealing away people's boats.

We went to check the boats, certain we would find them all safely stowed, but sure enough, when we did the count there was one canoe missing. We counted and then counted again until, eventually, we had to admit the lake had taken one. Of course, all kind of blame-gaming started, but ultimately, we all agreed that the fault lay not in the current but in ourselves and so we ought to take responsibility. It seemed only logical at that point that we should go and find the canoe before anybody else figured out it was missing.

The plan was for the counselor and I, the same rugged outdoorsman who had rescued and cooked my fish that night, to paddle out in our canoes, locate the lost vessel, and tow it back to shore. He somehow convinced me this would be perfectly safe. After the way he had helped me land the iconic fish, I was inclined to believe him. It was a calm lake on a moonlit night in the middle of nowhere. What could possibly go wrong?

And so, off I paddled, alone, into the darkness, listening to the swoosh of every paddle stroke. I soon found myself in a remote section of the lake. The water was like hand-blown glass shimmering in the light of the full moon. The stillness enveloped me completely. I felt peaceful and connected to nature in a way that I had never experienced before. Suddenly, I was one with the moonlight and the water and the vast tranquility of the forest. I have never forgotten that feeling. Which is remarkable because it lasted no longer than a few rare and immortal moments before my imagination kicked in—on steroids.

What were the odds of this counselor, Nature Boy, leaving canoes so carelessly close to the lake that they had floated away? I looked around and realized I was idling in foreign waters. I'd never seen this part of the lake before. Why had I paddled out here? He told me to do it. He told me it was safe. Maybe this was all just a ruse to lure me out onto the water while he slaughtered the slumbering canoers back at camp. Then, when I wandered back, tired and disoriented from lack of sleep, it would be my turn to meet the reaper. Of course, it was obvious. This was all a malevolent ploy, hatched by a monster. How could I have been such an idiot? Suddenly, I heard a loud bang, and then a shriek of joy echoed across the lake. Nature Boy had found the lost canoe.

Years later, it was very strange to discover myself suddenly longing for a reconnection with the great outdoors given my checkered history with Mother Nature. I was going through a divorce, which I guess is another time when men wander off into nature to test themselves, to see if they still measure up. This time, I was determined to come away with the upper hand.

It was during this period of my life that I began reading and becoming fascinated with Native American literature and Eastern philosophy. The Native Americans talked about their connection with nature and the cycles of creation. They believed that nature is embedded in us from the very beginning and its seasons are hardwired. The trouble is that for centuries we white folks have chosen to ignore it, evidently, at our peril.

I began to realize that most of Western civilization, pretty much from the get-go, had looked at nature as something to be conquered and exploited for our own benefit. We characterized our encounters with Mother Nature as a battle to be won. The Native Americans didn't see it that way. They saw themselves as stewards of the earth and intertwined with the Great Spirit. This resonated with me. I longed to be connected to something larger than myself, to the cycle of life.

Words You Can Take to the Bank

"

ANCIENT WISDOM FROM
THE FIRST AMERICANS (AND A RUSSIAN, TOO)

We must try to use the pipe for mankind, which is on the road to self-destruction… This can be done only if all of us, Indians and non-Indians alike, can again see ourselves as part of the earth, not as an enemy from the outside who tries to impose its will on it. Because we . . . also know that being a living part of the earth, we cannot harm any part of her without hurting ourselves.[24]
—*Lame Deer*

When you are in doubt, be still, and wait; when doubt no longer exists for you, then go forward with courage. So long as mists envelop you, be still; be still until the sunlight pours through and dispels the mists—as it surely will. Then act with courage.[25]
—CHIEF WHITE EAGLE, *Ponca*

Humankind has not woven the web of life. We are but one thread within it. Whatever we do to the web, we do to ourselves. All things are bound together. All things connect.[26]
—CHIEF SEATTLE, *Duwamish*

Drive nature out of the door, and it will fly in at the window.[27]
—FYODOR DOSTOEVSKY

I wanted more than anything to understand what being in harmony with creation felt like. I longed to let go, surrender the battle, stop trying to make things better. I think I felt this so intensely because, as I said, I was going through a divorce; I was laying down a burden and walking away. I felt liberated, almost weightless. I wanted more of that feeling, so when I saw the brochure about the outdoor leadership program, sea kayaking on the Baja Peninsula, I thought back to that moment at midnight in that canoe, and I went for it, hook, line, and sinker.

My boss told me I was crazy and should take a beach vacation instead. I insisted that this experience would teach me something about being a leader. And it did, right from the beginning, because finding my way from Cincinnati, Ohio, to a small beach town in Baja was no small feat. I had to fly to San Diego, and then catch a connection to Mexico, and then get on a Mexican bus and feel my way to the beach. It was daunting.

I landed in San Diego only to discover that my flight to Mexico had been canceled. I called the people at the leadership school, who said, well, get the next flight, which wasn't until the following day. This all sounded very shaky to me. But in the meantime, I had an entire day on my own in San Diego. By the end of that day, I thought to myself, why am I leaving? Why would I fly down to some random village on the Baja Peninsula when San Diego is so fine? Maybe I should listen to my boss and just kick back for a few days where there's reliable air conditioning.

I did get on the plane to Mexico the next day, and then I got on the Mexican bus headed for the beach. I memorized the route so I could find my way back. I even considered dropping crumbs out the bus window—I didn't want to get stranded. I got off at the last stop, stepped onto the beach, walked down a few hundred yards, and there they were, just like they told me. There were 10 of us, middle-class white Americans, men and women. Everybody had something they wanted to confront in their lives, and at a certain point on the trip, every one of us would come face to face with it.

Our guides were kids, a guy and a girl in their twenties out for adventure and, I think, up for helping a bunch of amateurs navigate the elements. It was hard to imagine what they could teach us about leadership, but they did know a little something about surviving in the wild. The first thing they taught us was how to find a smooth rock to use instead of toilet paper. The stock on smooth rocks shot through the roof on the spot.

Each day we hiked and climbed and kayaked. The guides showed us miracles of creation, and of course at times we also experienced the toughness of the great outdoors. Every afternoon we searched for a campsite for the night, and every time I noted that their guidance became patchier and the quality of our lives much less pleasant. It got harder and harder to imagine that this was all just bad luck.

One night our guides told us to bed down in a hollow that was completely infested with gnats. Yet you walked five yards out to where they were sleeping and, just like magic, no gnats. Then, there was the night of the scorpions. They led us into the middle of a field of smooth rocks. We figured we had hit the jackpot. A level surface to sleep on and as many smooth rocks as you could carry. Until one guy kicked over a rock in the night, only to discover that scorpions were hiding under every smooth stone. "Don't kick the rocks!" the counselor yelled, helpfully, from 10 yards off, safe and well away from the scorpions. I looked up and there was that full moon again, but where was my moment of peace with the world? I slept the rest of the night with one eye open.

On the fourth day, Caleb, one of our guides, announced that we would climb up to a summit where we'd find a beautiful oasis with crystal-clear water and probably even a couple of forest nymphs waiting for us with refreshments. He was really selling the hike. We were thrilled! We talked about what it might be like. I imagined that beautiful oasis. I dreamed about all of us, lounging and drinking the crystal-clear water and nibbling grapes... But first, we had to get to the top.

We approached a rock wall and scrambled up onto the ledge, not thinking about how high it was, and not looking down, only looking up toward that leafy oasis we knew was on top. After a tough climb and with a groan of exhaustion, I threw myself up onto the summit, stood up, and found myself looking into the oasis. Except it wasn't an oasis, it was a dirty scum-filled swamp littered with the half-desiccated corpses of prehistoric dead things. No grapes, no forest nymphs. Just dust and bones.

To say that I was disappointed would be an understatement. And I wasn't alone. We turned like a pack of hungry dogs on our guide, who seemed to see only the humor in the situation. He swore that this festering depression had once been a fertile valley. I wasn't interested in his explanations. I was already thinking about how I was going to get down, because there appeared to be no exit.

Our know-it-all guide seemed nonplussed. "We'll just climb down the same way we climbed up," Caleb said casually, but I could tell he was nervous. I looked down and felt dizzy. This is when I learned that looking up at your goal at the top of a peak looks a lot different in reverse.

Several of us discussed the idea of calling in an airlift. We looked around to find a place where a helicopter might land but none of us had brought a phone. Caleb the spin doctor was chock full of pep talks about how easy the descent would be. He would go first, he explained, and then he'd simply point out the good handholds and footholds to coach us down, one at a time.

His plan made sense, but he had already left me in a field of gnats and a den of scorpions, and now had got us stuck at the top of a scorched and polluted pass with no exit plan. If I learned anything on that trip, it was to know who your friends are, and I was beginning to have serious doubts about Caleb.

A couple of the braver souls began the intrepid trip down. Nobody died, which was a plus, but I wasn't budging. Finally, when all hope of an air rescue had been extinguished, it was my turn. My mom always told me, never give into peer pressure, but now I was alone at the top. Everyone was waiting on me at the bottom—it's not like I could say no. I started lowering myself down over the cliff, in waterlogged sneakers, with Caleb yelling from the bottom as I negotiated every crumbling inch of the rock face. And then, while I was balanced on a narrow ledge, my foot started slipping...and I froze.

"Mick, trust me, your foot will hold," Caleb yelled. "Just take the next step, you won't fall. I promise you won't fall." I didn't believe him. Why would I? No matter how he put it to me, I could not and would not move.

Finally, a voice spoke to me, and it wasn't Caleb's. It was my own and it said, *Mick, listen to the kid. You have to step down, your foot will hold.* I slowly moved my other foot to a sturdy ledge and from there was able to inch my way down to the bottom. Even to this day, I cannot find the words to adequately describe the relief and joy I found at the bottom of that rock face. We all celebrated our heroic journey in a moment of communion that only comes when you have looked into the rock face of death and laughed. As we walked away, I glanced back at the rock, filled with the pure joy of survival.

Later, one of the women on the trip showed me a picture she had taken with her trusty polaroid of my hair-breadth escape from the imminent deadly breach. She had caught me in that terrifying moment, hanging off a narrow ledge with my foot slipping, and had somehow managed to capture the entire face of the wall too, which showed how far I would have fallen if my foot hadn't held. Had I slipped, had I fallen, I realized that I would have plunged an entire four feet.

I was embarrassed when I took in the true reality of what my situation had been, how trivial the drop really was, but this is also the day that I learned about the difference between perceived risk and actual risk. I would draw on this lesson many times over when it came to the market. My first lesson, helpfully, came near the same time that I intrepidly faced down the awesome abyss from my four-foot ledge.

The perilous four-foot drop

In a turbulent market, ignoring real risk can sink you

Back in the late seventies and early eighties, inflation was skyrocketing over 10% and interest rates were over 15%, the result of which were major spikes in gold and oil prices. Naturally, the underlying stocks in oil and gold followed these trends and were one of the few places where investors were finding big profits, and phenomenal, titan-level success. After a decade of unexciting incremental returns in stocks and bonds, investors fell in love with these hard assets that were delivering in very dramatic ways.

Being young and new to the business, I also became infatuated with the trends of the moment, and so I particularly enjoyed following the portfolio of one of our larger clients who was heavily invested in a company called Dome Petroleum.[28] The client had purchased Dome long before my time, but I could see from the history that the investment had been a reliable and comfortable one for him. Then, Dome discovered a new oil reserve and was off to the races. The stock shot through the roof. The client's investment of several hundred thousand dollars soon became several million. Then Dome discovered even more oil, and the rally plunged ahead at breakneck speed. We were all thrilled and cheering like mad from the stands like we were at a horse race, which for all intents and purposes, we were. Our client became even more self-satisfied and confident when Wall Street analysts confirmed how wonderful this investment had become.

I was so used to hearing fantastic news about Dome's performance that when I heard one of the partners suggesting to the client that we should sell off some of the Dome stock, I was shocked. And I wasn't alone. The client was appalled, declared the partner's advice "nonsense," and held on to his position.

Later, I pulled the partner aside and asked him why he had given the client that advice. He explained to me that the client's investment in Dome had become his largest holding. What used to be a speculative stock in the portfolio was now larger than his more conservative core holdings, in other words not exactly "nonsense."

It made good portfolio sense, therefore, to reduce the Dome holding because the stock still had elements of risk, in fact, probably more than most because of the dramatic run up in the price. What was once a hidden gem was now quite popular, and this made the stock more vulnerable if the company disappointed or if the earnings faltered. Flavors of the month were highly dependent upon public perception of risk.

I thought he made good sense. His arguments convinced me, but the client wasn't having it. He thought the partner crazy for suggesting that he sell off even a little of his most lucrative position, and in the short run, it looked as if he was right—the stock rallied more over the next several months. Despite feeling beat up, the partner kept at it, and eventually got the client to agree that if the stock rallied further, they would cut back their holding modestly, and at least take part of their initial investment out of it.

Then, that fateful summer while the client was away on vacation, Dome rallied even more. As they had agreed, the partner sold a mere $25,000 out of what was now a multi-million-dollar position. The client returned, furious, having conveniently forgotten about the agreement. He came close to demanding that the firm buy back their stock and pay the capital gains taxes to boot, though ultimately, he eased up. But he did not let the partner forget as Dome rallied even further into the stratosphere. The idea of additional sales of Dome stock was now officially off the table.

It was about this time that changes were beginning to occur in the markets that were so profound that the economy would be feeling the impact for the next 40 years. They are still reverberating even as I write this. The combination of the monetary policy set by the Federal Reserve and the lower taxes of President Reagan's early policy appeared to help spur the economy while eventually lowering inflation.[29] After a recession that began in 1981, August of 1982 witnessed another explosion and this time it was in the financial markets.[30] Not oil and gold, but paper.[31] The stock market took off like a shot and guess what else happened? Dome and other oil stocks began to falter.

Perceiving a dramatic change in the market is so hard because we mostly focus on near-term events and rarely take a step back to look at the big picture. We can become mesmerized by past trends and unwilling to believe that a sea change is happening, and this can make us slow to hedge our bets.

This was the case with our client and Dome Petroleum. When the markets took off, buoyed by lower interest rates and an improving economy, a completely different group of stocks began to lead the market. The prices of gold and oil were no longer advancing, and their stock prices reflected this.

This shift marked the beginning of the glory days on Wall Street, which would set the stage for the many excesses of the eighties to come. But in the early days of this shift, no one imagined the riches that were to come or the personalities that would emerge and later live on as legend in movies like *The Wolf of Wall Street*.[32] No longer were oil[33] and gold[34] stocks the darlings of Wall Street, but rather a combination of consumer, technology, healthcare, and cyclical stocks reigned supreme. Oil and gold stocks peaked and then began a long decline.[35] Dome began its inevitable trek back to where it started.

When something is ready to implode, get out of the way

It's amazing to observe the psychology of a stock imploding and to watch investors completely freeze, unable to take any action to help themselves, much like the way I froze on the ledge that day. Always there is the look back, the hoping and wishing that if we just get the stock back up a few points, then we'll sell.

Few investors really believed that oil and natural resources could be on a long-term decline that would stretch for many years. This is when I learned that we should never discount what seems impossible because the impossible could be right around the corner. In fact, often if we just looked far enough back in history, we would see evidence that those things we thought could never happen, have happened before! Oil and natural resources have always traded in cycles and the argument that this time is different is a very costly phrase, especially, as it turned out, for this client.

We watched Dome Petroleum deliver disappointment after disappointment. We talked constantly of the best time and strategy to finally reduce the position but always the stock was too low and there was too much hope that it would rally or reclaim its past success. Dome eventually went the way of so many darlings of the oil bubble and became a mere footnote in Canadian business history and we never sold another share until it was nearly out of business. What the client was ultimately left with after riding a stock from a rally of almost 20-fold, turning hundreds of thousands of dollars into millions, was not much more than the mere $25,000 that the partner had forced them to sell, which he nearly fired us for! What I received were several lessons that I hope I never forget.

Surfing the market requires good balance

There is a reason that we diversify stocks in a portfolio. It is because we accept that future predictions are always fraught with error, no matter how astute we are. By diversifying a portfolio, we reduce the risk of any one stock hurting us too badly. If we are humble enough to admit that we simply do not have enough information to know everything about the future direction of any holding, then we will never allow an over-reliance on one stock to ruin us.

Dome Petroleum started out as a small position in a portfolio because the client knew it was a small company with much uncertainty and risk. He eventually confused a rising price with a reason to gain more certainty. A better strategy would have been to slowly reduce the position as it increased, perhaps not always bringing it to a small position but at least not letting it dominate the portfolio. This would have meant selling the stock numerous times along the way and fewer profits when it got to its high, but the discipline would have forced us to take profits out and lessened the ultimate risk and loss.

This strategy, as you saw in my story, gets a lot of pushback from folks who have fallen in love with their favorite holdings. What I am arguing for is a balanced approach.

You may love Apple or Microsoft and it's true that they have done fantastically well and appear to have no major downside, but that doesn't mean you should never take a little off the table.

IBM used to be the dominant technology stock[36] but has been a disappointment for years. Woolworth[37] and Eastman Kodak[38] were once the darlings of Wall Street: the former no longer exists and the latter is currently mired in losses.

Any stock is at some point vulnerable and when stocks are rallying on good news it is nearly impossible to predict the ultimate peak in prices, so it is best to reduce large positions over time. Selling off a portion of your high-performing assets frees up funds to buy something else, perhaps a new seed that can also grow large and abundant. And if, after you sell a little, the stock continues to rise, cheer up, you still have plenty of that stock to prosper with!

Don't get mad, get even

Naturally, any time a stock drops after a big run, there is the urge to believe that our good luck can't possibly have ended and that the run will continue. This is usually a reasonable reaction, and a normal correction can often allow investors who have not owned the stock to buy in or allow those with small positions to buy more. I am not arguing for across the board stop losses for every stock, or automatically selling given a certain percentage decline. However, if a stock moves severely downward and is significantly out of step with the market, it's important to know when to draw the line and create a stop loss.

In the case of Dome, the sales might have occurred after at least a 50% drop, which would have been significantly out of step with the market, and hard to take given the pride the client had in the stock. But eventually it would have helped to maintain a large portion of the profits from the holding and allowed the client to then move on to other holdings that could also have added value.

There is always another choice, and we don't have to be locked into the stocks we own. In this case, the great boom for oil and gold was ending but another bull market for stocks was just beginning—a rally that would perform well over the course of many years and increase nearly tenfold. The choices were plentiful as we were stuck watching Dome Petroleum disappear.[39]

This story ends with the client just being mad—mad at us and mad at himself. Being angry at us was a curious reaction considering we tried to get him to sell a portion of his Dome stock numerous times. But this is human nature. When bad things happen, we want somebody to blame. But anger is a costly emotion in the market. Every time we do something that costs us money and get angry about it is a squandered opportunity to learn an important lesson. And one of the lessons I would remember as I reflected on that rock-climbing experience years later is to be able to acknowledge the difference between real risk and perceived risk.

The thing that I have learned is that when we don't accept the lessons that fate and the market are trying to teach us, we are bound to repeat them, whatever the price.

My old boss used to say that no one rings a bell when the tide turns, and that is surely true whether it be in the markets or in our personal lives. It's up to each of us to observe and decide whether a market move is a decisive sea change or simply an adjustment in the current trend. It's up to us to perceive accurately whether a decline is a forty-foot plunge, or only a four-foot drop. When we use time and patience to our benefit, when we aren't in the throes of panic or denial, we can detect the difference between a perceived risk and a real one, act accordingly, and save ourselves.

Lessons I learned from Mother Nature about real risk and perceived risk

1. **It is easy to confuse a real risk with a perceived risk and often our emotions are too easily influenced by whatever fear jumps to our minds most strongly.** But it pays to take a moment to reflect on whether a situation is genuinely risky and has high odds of hurting us or whether it just seems scary and has low odds of happening. Falling off that cliff in Mexico seemed quite scary, but the real risk of injury was low considering the four-foot drop. The risk of losing money in Dome Petroleum seemed ridiculous to our client but that was a real risk that can happen to almost any holding. So, we should consider this possibility when forming positions in our portfolio. By simply diversifying and taking money out of big winners we can eliminate this real risk, at least with our investments.

2. **If we invest long enough, we will thankfully catch a big winner from time to time.** This is great for our balance sheet but is not a time to use our benign neglect strategy. Taking a little off the table reduces the chance that this winner can

turn around and be our biggest loser. Selling a little from time to time allows us to diversify into other potential winners. It doesn't mean we are rooting against this great holding or hoping for it to go down. After all, we still likely own a lot of it, but it does mean we are less vulnerable to a surprise to the downside.

3. **Like Mother Nature, the market can be vicious and unforgiving.** However, we can navigate this issue by doing the little things right to help ride out the storms. Check to be sure that canoes are pulled up on shore before setting up camp. Don't knock over rocks in a scorpion-filled beach. Remember that desert oases only exist in *mythical* tales, and finally, don't go wandering up cliffs in the middle of Mexico with waterlogged sneakers. Take little victories by trimming big winners—this money can be used for potential other winners and in the event of a surprise drop or change of trend, this may be the best profits you will have taken.

CHAPTER 4

THE MAN WHO DID EVERYTHING WRONG

And the Man Who Did Everything Right

"War? Who wrote down 'war'?!" And the speaker looked around the room implying some idiot wrote down war.

I was the idiot in question. I slunk down in my seat. I was attending an economists' luncheon and though I was no great fan of economists, I found every bit of information potentially valuable. And it was usually fun to gather with other advisors, especially whenever someone else agrees to pick up the tab. So I went, thinking to have a nice lunch and expand my knowledge without making a fool of myself. I had apparently failed on that score.

Fred was a celebrated economist visiting Louisville to share his views on the future of the economy and the market. He had passed around notecards and asked us each to write down where we thought interest rates and other market signposts might end up by the end of the year. He also asked us to write down what we thought might be the biggest surprise of the year. On my notecard, I wrote 'war' and for some reason that really tickled the expert.

"War! Boy, that's a new one," Fred chortled from his seat. "I ask this question everywhere I go, and believe me that's a lot of places, and nobody has ever come up with war. Boy, that is rich," and then he paused—another pause! The silence seemed to go on for minutes, everyone looking around and it became obvious he wasn't giving up until he found me, so I raised my hand. About 20 faces turned immediately toward me, half in astonishment, half relieved that the idiot was me and not them.

"Were you joking?" Fred asked me, drawing his syllables out long and then clipping them up at the end like a fishhook. "How do you imagine a war happening in America this year? Maybe you were envisioning something abroad? Like Chile or Argentina?" Everyone stared, waiting for my answer. I began to sweat. I couldn't take the easy road out Fred had offered me. I couldn't have located Argentina or Chile on a map if you paid me.

Thankfully, after my own excruciatingly long pause, a pause my boss would have been proud of, the simple answer came to me. "Well, Fred, you asked for a surprise, didn't you?" I flashed him my sincerest smile. "I have no idea why we would end up in a war. That's why it would be a surprise." Mercifully, Fred moved on. He'd had his fun with me, and I was forgotten. I'm pretty sure, though, that many in that room will have thought back to that awkward moment when, three months later, in September of that very year, the planes hit the World Trade Center and America went to war.

Here's the thing I've learned about surprises. They come as a surprise. And they are an unavoidable part of the market and, of course, our lives. As I had tried to explain to Fred all those years ago, surprises emerge improbably out of the blue and make us all look like idiots. But if we're prepared, we can grow from them in ways that predictions can never offer because we have to pivot in the moment and in doing so, we learn firsthand how well we've prepared for the impossible.

I had predicted the unpredictable war that came upon us in 2001, but did I act on this possibility? Did I warn my family? Sell my stocks? No. My prediction was just a fun and somewhat embarrassing story about how stupid I looked at an economists' luncheon, until the impossible happened on that horrible day.

Inspiring Words You Can Take to the Bank

THE FOLLY OF FORECASTS

Men, it has been well said, think in herds. It will be seen that they go mad in herds, while they only recover their senses slowly, and one by one.[40]
—CHARLES MACKAY

My life has been filled with terrible misfortunes, most of which never happened.[41]
—MICHEL DE MONTAIGNE

Thousands of experts study overbought indicators, head-and-shoulder patterns, put-call ratios, the Fed's policy on money supply...and they can't predict markets with any useful consistency, any more than the gizzard squeezers could tell the Roman emperors when the Huns would attack.[42]
—PETER LYNCH

The fact is that although there are always things to worry about, seldom do the things we fret about actually occur. It's always the one thing you don't predict, the one detail you forgot to attend to that ends up coming back to haunt you. It's also hard to predict whether a particular event will turn out to be a negative or a positive in the long run. Only time will tell you that.

Sometimes good fortune comes to the party disguised as bad luck

Often, when I am looking down the long nose of a down market, I think back to my first divorce. I got married fairly young because I thought getting married was what I was supposed to do. I thought it was what my parents wanted of me, what life expected of me as a responsible grownup. So, naturally, when my girlfriend said marry me or I'm leaving, I married her. Then, when I realized I was miserable, I started to worry. I worried about everything. I didn't do anything, I just worried and questioned myself.

Why was I unhappy? How was I going to get through my life when my future looked so grim? How could I take control of my life and find joy again without disappointing everybody? If my marriage fell apart, what would my parents say? What would my friends and colleagues think of me? Would I ever fall in love again or would I be alone for the rest of my life? When I looked into the future, I forecasted fear—fear of making my own decisions, fear of taking on challenges, fear of failing, and even fear of succeeding and having it feel hollow.

About a year or so later, my wife let me know that she was ready to have children. In her usual fashion she said, we are going to have children or I'm leaving you. Well listen, I can't really blame her. It worked the first time, and I think she fully expected the same result. Why wouldn't she? I too expected the same result, only I wound up surprising us both. "Sure, I want kids in my life," I heard myself telling her, "but it must be with someone that I love, and this is not a relationship built on love. So, you may as well leave."

That day I gave life a chance to surprise me. And instead of all the terrible things I'd imagined about getting divorced, I found joy. I found exhilaration. My gray life turned to technicolor. All my fears had been unfounded. I had been running from a fantasy. And so, I didn't mourn, I celebrated. What a wonderful surprise to realize I could face my fear, make hard decisions on my own behalf, and flourish. This discovery has helped me enormously in life, and in business.

Now I look at the inevitable surprises of life and the market as windows of opportunity rather than a crisis. When the unexpected happens, reacting out of fear is just about the worst thing that you can do.

The man who did everything wrong

All I remember about meeting Dr. Price for the first time is that he was good and angry. I mean he was hopping mad. He had just retired, and he had hired a prominent Cincinnati investment firm (not ours) to manage his money. Their strategy had been to make big bets with their portfolios, and they immediately put 100% of Dr. Price's holdings into long bonds. What many people don't realize is that contrary to long-standing popular opinion, bonds are not all that safe. There is a lot of risk inherent in long bonds depending on which direction inflation and interest rates head. They can be just as volatile as stocks.

Stock prices and bond prices often exist in an inverse ratio, so bonds can act as a good diversifier when stock prices fall. But in an inflationary environment or if stocks rally, interest rates can rise causing bond prices to fall. I don't believe the Doc understood this when he allowed his investment firm to place all his assets in long bonds, but he surely learned it the hard way when interest rates rose. Inside of six months, Dr. Price's million dollars had declined substantially, and boy was he mad about it.

What did Dr. Price do next? He fired the esteemed Cincinnati firm, pulled out of there lock, stock, and barrel, and hired us. This was not an ideal scenario for taking on a new client. You generally don't want new clients to be angry and reactive and inclined to blame their advisors for their losses. We tried to explain to him that the losses were paper tigers. They could be recouped when the bond market turned around, which it usually does, or when the bonds eventually matured. It was just going to take time. But Dr. Price was not a good patient.

We advised Dr. Price to play the long game and take a balanced approach, leaving some of his money in long bonds while diversifying into other types of investments. This meant we would be selling a portion of his long bonds to buy short-term bonds and some stocks. To prevent a surprise that might result in his wrath being turned upon us, we hedged our bets by explaining that over the near term it was unpredictable how the market would act. If we moved slowly and thoughtfully, however, we assured him that any short-term losses would likely be recouped over the long term.

Unfortunately, karma was not on Dr. Price's side. All through that summer interest rates continued to rise, which hurt us as we tried to sell off his bonds to build out his stock portfolio. We were selling low and buying high, and by the fall we had only bought a small portion of our target for stocks. Then the October crash came along, Black Monday, 1987, which saw stock prices decline about 22% in a single day.[43]

Although his allocation to stocks was still low, Dr. Price got angry all over again, only this time he was mad at us. The remaining long bonds the other firm had purchased for him actually helped his portfolio, adding to his frustration, and the stocks that we had bought for him declined, as did his opinion of us. Dr. Price had seen enough. He fired our firm and told us that he intended to put all his money into short-term CDs because he was through with investments, through with advisors, and through with risk. Of course, buying CDs at that time was, again, the exact wrong thing to do. As soon as he converted his portfolio out of stocks, the stock market hit bottom and rebounded. It went on to make great gains over the next 10 plus years, profits that Dr. Price likely never enjoyed.

What happened to Dr. Price could have happened to anyone who made rash, fearful decisions during that turbulent time or made big portfolio bets without understanding the risk of their investments. Dr. Price's initial decision to allow his original firm to make such a large bet exposed him to too much risk, and then that risk snowballed when the market hit rocky waters. He did the wrong thing at the wrong time at every turn because he was reactive. He was always coming from behind the eight ball. He did not have the confidence of his position. He was playing with anxious money, and anxious money is neither agile nor resilient and is likely to panic.

I would argue that Dr. Price could have avoided disaster if he had been prepared for the possibility of short-term losses and had learned that no matter what happened, he was able to do what was necessary to recoup and survive long term. That is how confident money behaves—investors who have thought out their risk profile in advance and don't panic because they are prepared for anything and are built for the long haul.

Parables You Can Take to the Bank
THE STORY OF THE CHINESE FARMER

Once upon a time there was a Chinese farmer whose horse ran away. That evening, all of his neighbors came around to commiserate. They said, "We are so sorry to hear your horse has run away. This is most unfortunate." The farmer said, "Maybe." The next day the horse came back bringing seven wild horses with it, and in the evening, everybody came back and said, "Oh, isn't that lucky. What a great turn of events. You now have eight horses!" The farmer again said, "Maybe."

The following day his son tried to break one of the horses, and while riding it, he was thrown and broke his leg. The neighbors then said, "Oh dear, that's too bad," and the farmer responded, "Maybe." The next day the conscription officers came around to conscript people into the army, and they rejected his son because he had a broken leg. Again, all the neighbors came around and said, "Isn't that great!" Again, he said, "Maybe."

The whole process of nature is an integrated process of immense complexity, and it's really impossible to tell whether anything that happens in it is good or bad—because you never know what will be the consequence of the misfortune; or, you never know what will be the consequences of good fortune.

—ALAN WATTS[44]

The man who did everything right

The first client I was to manage on my own was another doctor and the opposite of Dr. Price. Allen and his wife Jane were the couple who did everything right. They came to our firm having recently retired and asked me to look over their assets. They had previously agreed to a balanced account that included some stocks, but they were now questioning the wisdom of holding on to their stock portfolio. Although I didn't think we should sell their stocks—and in hindsight, their instincts were correct—luckily, I did the next best thing, I listened.

Jane and Allen had grown up during the Depression. Their families were both from Dayton, Ohio, and part of a working class that thrived in the Roaring Twenties. This tremendous growth and innovation followed just after a very dark period for the country, which included World War I and the first global pandemic. In addition, in 1913, the year that Jane and Allen were both born, Dayton had suffered the greatest natural disaster in Ohio history. The flood brought 20 feet of water into the city, killing 300 people, and costing over $100 million in damages, or over $2 billion in today's dollars.[45] But by the early 1920s, things had begun to turn around for Dayton and the American economy.

Allen's dad worked for a well-known entrepreneur who founded one of several companies that were flourishing in Dayton at the time. Other examples were John Patterson, who founded NCR with the cash register,[46] and Charles Kettering,[47] who invented the automobile starter and much more. Bright new, labor-saving technology companies were springing up all over the Midwest, bringing new convenience and ease to the average middle-class American home and new profits to American businesses.

For the first time, fueled by the optimism of post–World War I America, people were buying new marvels like refrigerators, freezers, and washing machines, and they were paying for them on credit. "Buy now, pay later" became the new American mantra.

But after these glorious years, things turned on a dime again for American families, including Jane and Allen's, when in 1929, the stock market crashed. Most people associate the crash with the beginning of the Great Depression. For most American families who did not own stock,[48] however, this was more of an isolated financial event that affected mostly the rich and did not directly impact the quality of life for the average person. The thing that did affect most Americans, of course, was the run on the banks over a year later, caused by people's loss of faith and optimism.

Watching an institution like the stock market tumble was terrifying. Americans had never seen a crisis like this before and hadn't even believed such a thing could happen. It caused most consumers to pull back, to stop spending on durable goods, and to lose faith in a brand-new credit system[49] that had suddenly imploded.

Certainly, there is enough blame to go around when it comes to the Depression.[50] Whether it be Herbert Hoover, who was President at the outset, or the Federal Reserve, which did not recognize the need to ease money, it was a perfect storm on many fronts. But the panic that people and companies felt, causing everyone and everything to contract, was surely a major contributor to the devastation that occurred in the 1930s.

Americans who grew up during the Depression came of age with the understanding that you couldn't rely on anything to last forever. Things could always slip away. Allen and Jane understood this. Yet rather than making them fearful, it seemed they remained hopeful and confident about the future—more reassured that life would work itself out, though they were always watchful and never forgot the lessons they had learned.

Granted, Jane and Allen had had a good life. Allen was a successful orthopedic surgeon and Jane took pride in raising their kids and keeping a wonderful home. Their lives were filled with the love they had for each other, and their family and their children all grew up to be successful. Yet, Jane and Allen never forgot the struggle they endured in their early lives, and it gave them strength and resilience.

They would often talk to me about the hardships that they and their families and neighbors had endured during the Depression. They had survived some of the darkest periods in our history and wanted to be sure that if another crisis came about, they would be prepared. They understood that everything moves through cycles, and they sensed intuitively that the stock market had been in an up cycle for a little too long. They told me they were worried about stocks. They feared that another turn of the wheel could be coming.

After listening to their concerns, I took a long pause, a pause that even my boss, the champion of long pauses, would have applauded. During my time out, it occurred to me to explain to them why their portfolio, even with their stock position, would be just fine over the long term. But as I looked at them, fortunately, my history lessons kicked in, and rather than dismiss their reservations I went in another direction entirely. I decided to address their concerns directly.

Instead of just telling them that we were well diversified and there was nothing to be afraid of, I considered the possibility of another crash. I proceeded to go through an exhaustive analysis of what would happen to their stock portfolio if the market crashed, just as it had done in 1929. And the truth was, because of their low allocation to stocks, based on their risk tolerance and long-term objectives, even in the event of another historic financial disaster, Jane and Allen would be okay.

I told them all of this. I showed them my charts and graphs and projections that illustrated how much they would still have, even after another crash, based on a low exposure to stocks and a balanced allocation to short and long bonds. After my presentation, they became comfortable with the plan. Ironically, just two weeks later, the market crashed, just as they had feared. I then had to face what I thought would be the unpleasant task of calling Jane and Allen and telling them that they had been right.

But there was encouraging news. When I priced everything out, I realized that their account was amazingly close to where I had estimated things would fall in this type of crash. As a result, they weren't mad at all. And they weren't frightened either. What a different call than the one made to Dr. Price that very same day. When I told Jane and Allen the bad news, they remained calm and positive. They told me they had loved my analysis, and in fact gave me credit for listening to their concerns. As a result, they had accepted the risk of potential decline if a crash occurred. And now, being braver than I expected, they told me that they wanted to buy stocks. This time I did listen and that's exactly what we did. We bought more stocks at the lows and Jane and Allen became very successful long-term clients.

I continued working for them for many years. We stuck to our plan, reduced stocks when the market had brought their allocation to higher levels and added stocks after significant declines. This allowed them to comfortably maintain their lifestyle and stay close to their original principal, even after many years of spending.

This experience once again demonstrated that by not doing anything spectacular you can still end up with a spectacular result! But in addition, the defining moment in 1987 showed me that when Jane and Allen had understood and accepted what type of risk they were assuming, it gave them the strong hands they needed to do the right thing when the markets became volatile.

MONEY CAN'T BUY YOU CLASS MOVIES

Wall Street (1987)[51]

DIRECTOR: *Oliver Stone*

STARS: *Michael Douglas, Charlie Sheen*

Oliver Stone's classic cautionary tale about the wages of greed and the true value of family is a great reminder that just because someone has a lot of money doesn't mean they are a good emotional investment. This is a fantastic snapshot of the supersonic eighties market on Wall Street, and the attitude that almost took us under.

The Wolf of Wall Street (2013)[52]

DIRECTOR: *Martin Scorsese*

STARS: *Leonardo DiCaprio, Jonah Hill, Margot Robbie*

Based on the true story of Jordan Belfort, Leonardo DiCaprio stars as the man who had too much and learns that even for titans of Wall Street, there is no free lunch.

The Bonfire of the Vanities (1990)[53]
DIRECTOR: ***Brian DePalma***
STARS: ***Tom Hanks, Bruce Willis, Melanie Griffith***
This Tom Wolfe novel adaptation shows the catastrophic events that happen to a Wall Street warrior when he winds up in the Bronx. This is a great reminder that Wall Street and Main Street, or in this case, The Cross Bronx Expressway, have very little in common and that even money men who look big on the bottom line shrink by comparison when the French cuffs come off.

So, let's compare these two doctors

What can we do to avoid becoming like the man who did everything wrong? Here's a few ideas to bear in mind:

1. **Understand your risk.** We must understand the risk of the assets in our portfolios. Looking back at how volatile different assets have historically been is not a perfect system, but it sure offers a valuable perspective. Had Dr. Price been made aware of the risk he was taking initially with all those long bonds, perhaps he would not have felt quite as angry when the price of bonds fell. Maybe then he wouldn't have made such volatile choices. .

2. **Never play with anxious money.** Avoid investing money you can't afford to lose. At some point it is inevitable that the market will fluctuate, and you will be tested. If you own too much, human nature is to panic; and when we panic, we usually make unfortunate decisions. We wind up freezing when we

should move or moving when we should freeze. Either way, my experience is in these instances we all tend to make the wrong decisions when we're frightened.

3. **Manage your expectations.** Once we make a bad decision, it is very hard to get back on the right track, so try not to make too many decisions. We don't need to predict every bull and bear market and the odds are we won't, so it's best to set up a good structure and then stick with it. Set your objectives for stocks and bonds at reasonable levels. Allow for the fact that volatility will happen and occasionally take advantage when markets are at extreme levels.

4. **Know your risk threshold.** The best way to prepare for a surprise in the stock market is to keep your allocation close to the target that meets your risk threshold. Of course, if your risk threshold is zero, that's a tough assignment, but most of us can accept some volatility in our portfolios. Ask yourself, what is it that would scare me into selling at market lows? What level of decline would cause me to think, uh oh, I have too many stocks? Determine your tolerance levels and respect those boundaries.

5. **Be patient.** Remember, when declines happen it can seem like the end of the world: Worldwide Pandemic! Planes Hit the Twin Towers! Financial Collapse! Reading headlines during a surprise event is unavoidable but not helpful to investors. Patience is your best friend in times like this. Even if we somehow bought stocks at the top of every cycle, somehow just had that perfect negative karma but also the patience to hold on, we would likely do just fine and significantly better than the person who panics, gets out of the market, and then is

never able to get back in.

6. **Stay humble.** It's important to keep in mind that we know very little about predicting the future. We can only use history and common sense to help guide our investments. We need to stay humble, and bear in mind that the so-called experts have no monopoly on predicting the future either, no matter what they say. None of us knows what will happen tomorrow.

CHAPTER 5

VICTORY IS A RELATIVE TERM

Why Success Is Always Incremental

"Timeout!"

My coach was fuming. We were losing bad. And by bad, I mean it was 91–24 against us with only about five minutes left on the clock. The only real question was whether we would let the other team put 100 points on the board, which rarely happens in high school basketball. Our imminent defeat was on an epic scale. Historic. Literally one for the record books. Equally, our opponents' victory was about to become legendary.

"Should we just walk off the court now and concede?" Coach asked, looking at each of us like he could see straight through to that mortifying scoreboard behind us. He was furious, surprisingly not at our performance, but at the other team who still had their starters in, trying to rub our noses in it. Suddenly, he turned and looked at me.

"What do you think, Mick?" I was speechless. Nobody cared what I thought about much of anything in those days, let alone basketball. I had spent most of the season warming the bench and was only on the team to fill the seventh player slot vacated by the last bench-warmer who had just graduated.

As a newly minted senior, I thought it might be fun to letter in something before I graduated, but I knew I was no Larry Bird. Not sure if I could have even made the starting lineup for most sixth grade teams. I had only played in a few games—ones when we'd already won or lost by a lot, and it didn't matter anymore. In fact, even in those moments people behind the basket were often diving for cover after I took a shot. There were some very talented players on our team playing that day. Why didn't Coach ask them their opinion? Why me?

Then I thought about it, and I realized that Coach and I had spent a lot of time together on that bench. He was very vocal during games, shouting in his instructions, cursing at the fumbled plays. And I had been listening. So, maybe he had turned to me in that moment because we had developed a relationship. I knew how he saw things. And he had learned a little about the way I saw things too. I could see how frustrated and discouraged he was. I wanted to help if I could.

"Why don't we at least try to hold them under 100?" I suggested. "I mean, at least we could do that much, right? They seem to want it pretty bad." Coach looked at me, and then I saw that familiar gleam flicker back to life in his eyes. He turned to the team.

"That's what we're going to do, boys! We're going to hold them under 100 just like Mick here said. We are going to stop them from hitting their mark, because you know they want it bad." I had been in the game because of the lopsided score but immediately Coach barked, "Starters, you're back in. Mick, you're back on the bench." Was I offended that Coach didn't put me into the game? No. I had already made my best contribution. I was content to let the starters do what they did best and make it happen out there on the court.

Back in the seventies when there was no shot clock, there was a thing called the four-corner play, which was a dribbling and passing strategy designed to eat up time. Teams tended to use this strategy when they were ahead on the scoreboard because it ran out the clock. We were now reimagining this strategy move and using it to run out the clock while we were behind. It was revolutionary, mind-blowing, and because the other team had not expected it, the plan appeared to be working.

The other team looked super mad. Their fans did too. After all, they had been screaming, "We want a hundred!" for quite some time. As you can imagine, those final few seconds were insane with excitement and anticipation, and in the end, we denied the opposing team that coveted 100 points on the board. Suddenly, their victory felt more like a loss and our defeat a triumph. A collective groan rose from the bleachers as the game clock signaled the end, and we charged off the court like champions. I think the fans even threw things at us. The final score was 99–28 against us, and we could not have been prouder. The team had never felt the thrill of victory more intensely.

Despite this lopsided win/loss, in the end our season didn't turn out too badly. We won about half our games that year, some quite impressively. But at the year-end banquet, when Coach talked about his favorite game, it was this one that he chose to lift up. He told us that we would remember it for the rest of our lives, and he was right.

All these years later, it is this game above all others that I most vividly recall.

Winning is about setting and celebrating achievable goals

Why was this win/loss so memorable? First, in that fateful game, we were clearly outmatched. From the outset we didn't have a chance, and sure enough, it showed. But in those furious final seconds, as the other team scrambled to get to 100, we brought our best, and the fight was suddenly even. We emerged victorious because we narrowed the aperture, we redefined our expectations, and went for an incremental win. Because we changed our perception of what winning meant, we were able to snatch victory from the jaws of defeat against all odds. The cumulative power of relative victories became clear for all of us on the court and in the bleachers that day.

Unfortunately, growing up in America, this is not a lesson we are taught very often. We are encouraged to go for the gold, to win full out, and we are disappointed when we don't achieve total and complete success. The idea that we have to slug it over the fence, swing for the bleachers, and win big every time makes it hard to appreciate the more gradual nature of real success in our adult lives. I see it in my fellow parents at little league baseball or pee wee football games. Living in California, I even see it at surfing competitions. I've watched little kids doggy paddling back to shore while their parents demand to know, "How could you miss that wave!"

It's not that the competitive instinct is bad—in fact that fierce sense of competition is fundamentally American. The trouble is how we define victory. It should never be about the strikeout in the bottom of the seventh that matters most, it's about the long game. It's about whether that kid has a passion or love for what they do and is open to learning important lessons about teamwork, mastery, discipline, collaboration, confidence, and endurance. That's success, not winning a pee wee surfing competition.

Most of us know this, but we get distracted by our desire for the huge win. We forget to keep our eyes on the real prize. We forget the value of relative victories—we forget this is supposed to be fun. And as we move into the world of wealth, that gets costly.

Inspiring Words You Can Take to the Bank

THE MONEY BALL

The investor's chief problem—and his worst enemy—is likely to be himself. In the end, how your investments behave is much less important than how you behave.[54]
—BENJAMIN GRAHAM

If you don't know who you are, this is an expensive place to find out.[55]
—ADAM SMITH (*pseudonym for George Goodman*)

I can calculate the motions of the heavenly bodies, but not the madness of people.[56]
—SIR ISAAC NEWTON

Success isn't permanent, and failure isn't fatal.[57]
—*Some say* MIKE DITKA, *but exact quote appears to be from a Budweiser beer commercial in the 1930s*

It really is about how you play the game

I learned once again how important relative victories can be to a person, a team, or even a community as a young advisor back in the ride-or-die eighties. We were meeting with one of our wealthier clients, who would typically bring an entourage with him: a coterie of bean-counters and other functionaries whose purpose I couldn't quite pinpoint. All I knew was he filled up the conference room every time he came to visit. On this particular day there was a new addition to the team, and when he introduced himself, I had to struggle not to gasp. His name was Joe, and he was the former president of a local savings and loan (S&L) that had collapsed. I'd heard that Joe had served time in jail as a result of his fiduciary negligence.

After the initial shock of seeing a headline in the flesh, and as I got to know Joe a little better, I realized that he was a gentle, intelligent, and kind-hearted man who had a solid perspective on the markets. He had entered the savings and loan business as a young man because he—much like the iconic George Bailey in the Capra Christmas classic, *It's a Wonderful Life*—wanted to help people achieve their goal of owning a home. This was why savings and loans had been created as an institution back in the thirties.

How S&Ls came to stand for Savings and Losses

The Depression had come to a bitter end and millions of Americans were returning home from World War II and looking to rebuild family life. Savings and loans[58] were firmly grounded in their communities and personally connected to their borrowers. The whole reason for their existence was to restore faith in the American Dream, and the financial institutions that helped to make that possible. This is what had inspired Joe to go to work in an S&L, and over the years, he was able to move up in the business to eventually become the bank's president.

So how could this man, who began his career thinking he could be another George Bailey and lift up his town, have gotten so far off track? In fact, in the mid eighties what happened to Joe and his S&L was just the tip of the iceberg. Over the next several years over 1,000 S&Ls would fail. For the final years of the eighties and well into the nineties, the S&L collapse screamed ahead.[59] One of the more famous episodes was Lincoln Savings, which eventually saw Charlie Keating go to jail but not before pulling in five senators, who, in different ways, interfered with the investigation. Another major S&L failure was Silverado Savings where Neil Bush was found to have breached his fiduciary duty.[60]

Untold millions were lost by depositors in the S&L crisis, and although much of the money was ultimately recovered, it left its mark, sowing suspicion about an institution that was created to restore trust. It was easy to assume, in the dynasty-driven, over the top culture of the eighties, that whoever was responsible for these lost savings were just bad people. But after getting to know Joe, I realized that things just weren't that simple. The situation was relative.

Certainly, fraud was at the center of many of these bank failures and many bank officers went to prison for good reason. In listening to Joe, though, what I began to realize is that it was an industry-wide inability to value relative victories that led to disaster, and not just Gordon Gecko/Wall Street-style greed.

The eighties were an era when excess and opulence ruled the culture.[61] Hair was huge, and so were the potential risks and profits available to investors. *Dynasty* and *Dallas*, featuring the destructive squabbles of generational wealth, were the biggest shows on TV. Donald Trump was perfecting *The Art of the Deal*[62] and Madonna was hitting the charts with *Material Girl*. You get the idea. So, while the goal of protecting depositors' money and making safe bets should have been the primary objective for the S&Ls, you can't blame them for experiencing a little FOMO (Fear of Missing Out).

The trouble was the government created the S&L system to promote homeownership for the working class. To achieve this, they paid lower-than-average interest rates on deposits, and therefore were able to offer lower-than-average mortgage rates to their customers.[63] Consequently, prior to 1982, there were regulations in place that prevented the S&Ls from lending money for eighties-style profit-generation investment vehicles, like commercial real estate, for example. They couldn't even offer their customers checking accounts.[64]

While everybody else was getting *Dynasty* rich, the S&Ls were stuck with a dwindling portfolio of low-interest mortgages as their only income source. By 1982, S&Ls were losing $4 billion a year.[65] Then along came deregulation, permitting S&Ls to use federally insured deposits to make risky loans. Suddenly, these staid, flannel-gray bankers went, as they say in Texas, hog wild. They were Icarus, flying too close to the sun with wings made of wax, before plummeting to earth with a price tag of about $150 billion to American taxpayers.[66,67,68] This is what happens when you fail to appreciate the value of relative victory and insist on going for the gold when your job is to simply finish the race.

THE REAL-VALUE-OF-A-DOLLAR MOVIES

It's a Wonderful Life (1946)[69]

DIRECTOR: *Frank Capra*

STARS: *Jimmy Stewart, Donna Reed, Lionel Barrymore*

Frank Capra's Christmas classic reminds us all that real generational wealth is built gradually over time and is measured by friends, family, community, and all things more valuable than the bottom line.

American Hustle (2013)[70]

DIRECTOR: *David O. Russell*

STARS: *Amy Adams, Christian Bale, Jennifer Lawrence*

Two con artists are forced into an FBI sting operation, based on the Abscam scandal in the 1970s, which brought down several politicians. It is a fun characterization of the era, especially the hair and dress of the characters. But through it all, as we are pulled into different personalities, it helps us realize that there is possibly some good and bad in all of us.

Swimming with Sharks (1994)[71]

DIRECTOR: *George Huang*

STARS: *Kevin Spacey, Frank Whaley, Michelle Forbes*

A young assistant in a big Hollywood agency will do anything to reach the top of the star ladder. Unfortunately, he has to get by the world's meanest boss, and ultimately realizes that reaching for the gold can put you in places you never intended to go.

I believe that a lot of the S&L fraud probably began as an attempt to cover up a bad investment in the credit markets. Most of these S&L presidents were no better traders than anyone else, but in their case, they were playing with depositors' money. Whether it was outright fraud or not, these actions resulted from an illusion of invulnerability when it came to market movement. Bankers ignored the relatively simple objective of protecting capital! If these giants of finance, whether that be Charlie Keating or my friend Joe, had stopped to consider the implications of their actions over the long run, I believe things would have gone dramatically differently for their banks and their depositors.

In the short run, great profits were made, but ultimately, great losses and jail terms were incurred for many not necessarily bad people, but certainly short-sighted people like Joe. I believe that Joe was a kind father and a generous person. But he lost sight of the end game and forgot to value his relative victories in life, which were many, and so ultimately lost track of who he was and what he stood for.

Fortunately, the town that Joe helped to grow and prosper remembered his generosity and help through the years, and in the end, he found a community willing to forgive. Joe had learned the hard way about what is truly important in the market and in life—loyalty, trust, and true friendship.

The 60% Solution

This relatively simple strategy can help keep it real in good times and bad. It's called the 60% solution—although we could use it for any allocation of stocks—and here's how it works. Suppose we determine that 60% in stocks fits our long-term objective, considering our risk tolerance and needs for cash and income. First, if we start with all cash, I tend to move slowly in building to the ultimate objective, sometimes over many months. If we move too fast, we risk regretting it if the market moves against us. By moving slowly, or "averaging in" as the expression goes, there is less chance that any move in the market will scare us.

Once we meet our 60% objective, we will find that nothing ever stays the same. As the market moves, we will see our allocation move up and down with it. The discipline I follow is that when the market moves higher significantly and we see our allocation naturally rise in sync to, let's say 65 or 70%, then it is time to take profits and reduce exposure back toward the 60% target. On the other hand, if the market dropped significantly to 50 to 55% then I would begin to increase exposure, again back to the 60% target.

In this way, we are always taking some profits when the market is higher and buying when the market is lower. But importantly, we are not trying to predict the future, nor are we trying to be heroes: we are being disciplined and sticking to our long-run objectives. Of course, being in the business, I have tried to anticipate significant moves in the market and have sometimes done so successfully, but ironically most of my best moves have occurred by just following this discipline, not trying to be too smart, and being satisfied with a relative victory!

And what about the money that is not in stocks? Of course, this money should be in safe assets, but what is safe may change over time. In a low-interest-rate environment, simply owning treasury bonds could provide risk because bond prices move in the opposite direction of interest rates, so if interest rates rise, bond prices may fall. A conservative strategy is to make a "ladder" of maturities so each year a bond comes due, and if rates rise there is an opportunity to keep reinvesting at the higher yields. Money market funds may not provide much in return like they did in years past but at least they don't decline when stock prices decline. These are often decisions to be made with an advisor, but knowing one's objective and being sure the advisor is meeting that objective is really the key to long-term success.

Rules for Safe Flying with Wax Wings

1. **Don't be lured in by aviators with a God complex**

   In every significant market decline—the 1987 crash, the dotcom debacle, the crash of 2008—you will always find Icarus-inspired investors who decide they want riskier investments to provide returns and wind up flying too close to the sun. But it's most often quality investments that come through in the end to sweep up the feathers and protect the investors' money from total destruction. So don't be lured in by advisors with a God complex. The market provides so many chances for relative victories and it is important to focus on those.

2. **Don't glide on the hot air of former fliers**

   Not a day goes by without a hedge fund manager, trader, or advisor going on some financial show and boasting about their record. We can almost always be certain that whichever number they are showing off about, it is relative to something we probably don't know about and is designed to show them off in their best light. We all must work hard to ignore the boasts and stay focused on our relative triumphs and our own better instincts.

3. **Keep your eye on the horizon line**

Stay focused on your long-term objectives. Most of my clients don't care so much about beating the S&P 500 every year. Mostly they want their fair share in good years, to not get blown away in bad years, and to have a good income in between. Over time we can look at different comparisons and they can see that, thankfully, we have achieved their financial goal, albeit sometimes in better fashion than others. But if measured against some hedge fund who happened to have a great six months, they would probably feel like our team did when Coach yelled timeout. The key is to set our goals wisely, make sure they are achievable and measurable, and then stay focused on that horizon.

4. **Don't compare your plane to a rocket ship**

In my mind, I never want to be worried about competing with investors who are shooting for the moon, with big margins of victory and defeat. Some aggressive investors are into that kind of risky elevation. They want to shoot their profits into orbit and then tell everybody about it when they succeed. They don't tell you about the times that they crashed to earth. This can sometimes make us conservative investors feel a little boring and like we are underperforming with our modest but reliable returns. But if you go back far enough, the market has shown us plenty of times that big risk-takers feel pain. If they are wired to accept the pain and hold on, things can work out well for them but if not, this kind of high flying usually leads to panic selling and losses that they will certainly not tell you about. The key is to focus on your goals and not be distracted by astronauts unless you are prepared to defy gravity with them.

5. **Make sure you can handle midair surprises without going into a death spiral**

   If some new surprise strikes when you are at cruising altitude, make sure you can handle the paper losses. For some that may mean 40% in stocks, for others, 80% or higher. We must, in the end, know ourselves and have the humility to realize how much loss we can survive psychologically before we would give up and sell.

CHAPTER 6

DON'T GET CAUGHT IN A ROMANCE WITH YOUR MONEY

There Is a Time to Stay and a Time to Go

I have often thought that investing at times can be comparable with falling in love. You get enraptured in the moment, overjoyed and dizzy with bliss. It's a wonderful feeling, and you think it will go on forever. And then, even when things start to trend downward, you look past it, you stay the course, because it's hard to let go of the euphoria. Therefore, and remember this and say it often, DO NOT FALL IN LOVE WITH ANY SINGLE INVESTMENT. You don't want to be making decisions based completely on euphoric feelings. It never ends well. I should know. I've been there.

Yes, even me with my background and extensive education and experience in market cycles and in marriages must be reminded of this from time to time. When you're in the grip of something that you adore, that you feel you can't live without, LOOK OUT. When you're infatuated and soaring on the wings of love, it becomes very difficult to remember that the rules still apply to you. And one of those rules is that nothing lasts forever—especially euphoria.

The market is not a candy store

Let me take you back in my history to a candy aisle of a grocery store, where I ended up one day in search of a sugar fix, shortly after my second divorce. My marriage of 22 years had just ended, so I was in that shell-shocked state, wandering aimlessly without a plan, and without a list. I was in the mood for something sweet, something comforting—something tasty and high in sugar and calories. I wandered in the direction of the Snickers fun-size bars, when I saw a beautiful woman walking toward me, and suddenly, that tingle I was looking for in the candy aisle took a new shape and form.

I glanced casually in her direction, trying to look nonchalant. I looked away, but when I looked back, she was staring right at me. Now, I am not accustomed to beautiful women staring at me. I am many things, but chick magnet is not one of them. So, I was curious. Why was she looking at me like that? I didn't know what she wanted.

"Haven't I met you somewhere before?" she said then, and I almost chuckled, despite myself. How many times had I used that same lame line and had women roll their eyes at me over my total lack of originality? Let's just say, more than a few. Still, she was extraordinarily beautiful, so I had to play along. I wasn't going to let opportunity pass me by.

"You look really familiar to me too," I said. Of course, I had no memory of her, but who wanted to split hairs? "We must know each other from somewhere. Where could we have met?"

We stumbled around for a bit then, trying to discover our points of possible intersection, which I really didn't think existed. She said that she had a daughter, so did I. I asked if her daughter might have played in the eight and under softball league with my daughter, but her daughter was 17. That wasn't it. Then I mentioned I had a son who was around her daughter's age, and a surfer, and then it clicked. She remembered my son, reminded me that her daughter and my son had gone to the same elementary school. And as it happened, the two of us had volunteered in the same class and had met each other many times. I was gob smacked. It wasn't a line. She was telling the truth!

It all came back to me in a rush. We did know each other from way back when, and she was as beautiful now as she was then. I remembered those days of volunteering and chatting with her in a friendly way. I also remember thinking at the time that I was happily married and made it a point to not take our friendly conversation any further. At the time, her beauty had made me think that only trouble would come from furthering our friendship. After a while, my wife met her too and all was pleasant and polite and completely above board. Then our kids grew up and moved on and I never saw her again. Until of course, this unexpected meeting in the candy aisle. We decided it must be kismet.

Given that we were both divorced now, I asked her if she'd like to get together for lunch, and she said yes. I couldn't believe my good luck. I walked out of that grocery store on air. That lunch began a whirl-wind romance beyond my wildest dreams. We spent long weekends together and spoiled ourselves at over-priced spas. We vacationed in the Hamptons and even explored Switzerland where her daughter had decided to go to school. Our kids met and all got along. My daughter adored her, and even my ex-wife liked her. It was a dream come true. Eventually, I asked her to move in.

And of course, this is when the clay feet on the pedestal I had built for her began to crumble. Surprised? Of course, you aren't, but I was. I tried to overlook the chips in her perfect patina. I wanted to keep feeling the rush of romance a little longer. The first problem arose when she told me that after raising her daughter on her own, she had dreams of traveling and living in Europe now that her daughter was in college. I have a daughter that I am raising half the time, who is not in college yet. Not even close. My two sons live close by, and I liked where I lived. I did not dream of living in Europe. I enjoyed travel too, maybe spend a week on the beach in Maui. Her idea of travel was two months on the Amalfi coast.

As time moved along, I began to discover that our personalities were as divergent as our vacation dreams. She could be intense and driven. I am mellow, laid back, and relatively content. Of course, at first those differences were a delight. We joked about how opposites attract. I did kind of remember my mom mentioning years back that the quirks you love about a person in the beginning often turn into points of contention. Her words echoed loudly in my mind as time went on.

I know this will surprise everyone, but gradually, the blush on the rose began to fade. It was replaced by the bitter taste of disappointed dreams and petty but chronic arguments. I remember us sitting on different sides of the couch, her fuming about something and me not remembering what I was supposed to apologize for. I remember thinking, *How did we get here? What happened to our fairy-tale romance?*

The answer, of course, is that fairy tales are fairy tales. They're like a ride in an amusement park—thrilling for a few moments, and then the experience is over unless you pay for another ride. I give her credit for knowing when the ride was done. She called it long before I did. She "stopped out" as we investors say, cut her losses, and moved away.

I was of course heartbroken. I grieved deeply, even though underneath it all I knew it was the right decision. It was so hard to let go of what I had imagined our life would be. I wonder, could I have ripped off the Band-Aid myself, knowing that the relationship was not healthy for either of us? To this day I'm still not sure.

For years, I had helped clients let go of stocks they were loath to sell out of sentiment. Who could not rip off the Band-Aid when it was clear it was time for them to do so. I was dismissive of their pain, but now here I was in a relationship going badly and I felt the same agonizing hesitation. I didn't let go until I was forced to. And it taught me something about why you should never, ever, fall in love with an investment. It's not the right state of mind from which to make financial decisions, and overstaying your welcome can be very, very costly.

Inspiring Words You Can Take to the Bank

66

MONEY CAN'T BUY YOU LOVE

A bull market is like sex. It feels best just before it ends.[72]
—BARTON BIGGS

Illusions commend themselves to us because they save us pain and allow us to enjoy pleasure instead. We must therefore accept it without complaint when they sometimes collide with a bit of reality against which they are dashed to pieces.[73]
—SIGMUND FREUD

Through error you come to the truth! I am a man because I err! You never reach any truth without making fourteen mistakes and very likely a hundred and fourteen.[74]
—FYODOR DOSTOEVSKY

Don't get blinded by the light—or the blight

When you're caught up in a market upswing, or a market plunge, or when you happen on to a sweet new opportunity with enormous promise, it's easy to get blinded by the light. We get caught up with our investments the same way that we get caught up in a great romance and go a little blind. It's only with time and distance that things become clear.

Early in my career I saw how emotions drove many people's relationship with money, in the late seventies, when the world was waking up from a decade-long bad dream. It's so easy in hindsight to see what was happening back then, but in the moment, none of us was aware that everything was about to change.

There was angst in the air. Crisis after crisis from the Vietnam War to the massacre at the Munich Olympics[75] had weighed the country down. Then of course there was Watergate and Nixon resigning, not to mention the worst recession since the Depression. There were impossibly long gas lines to buy impossibly expensive gas during the oil shortage. The seventies ended with more than 50 Americans being taken hostage in Iran, and then the helicopter that was sent to rescue them crashed. No question about it. The American Dream was taking a real drubbing, and people were fed up.

Not surprisingly, a successful movie of the 1970s was *Network*. The famous refrain from Howard Beale, the populist protagonist of the film, was, "I'm mad as hell and I'm not going to take it anymore!" This surely summed up in a sentence what most Americans were feeling then, and, chillingly, seem to be feeling now.

This national malaise was naturally reflected in the stock and bond markets at the time. The Dow Jones Industrial Average was up a disappointing 5%—for the entire decade![76] This was accompanied by a total debacle in the bond market as interest rates rose dramatically, reflecting the rise in inflation. Long treasury yields that started the decade at around 7.5% traded in 1981 at close to 16% and CD rates were close to 18%.[77] Mortgage rates that started the decade at around 7.5% topped 18% by the early 1980s.[78] Bonds had lost so much value in the seventies they were nicknamed "Certificates of Confiscation."[79]

Some of this anger boiled over at a White Sox game in Chicago in 1979. Between the games of a doubleheader, management decided to allow a local radio host to blow up disco records in the stadium as a promotion.[80] Instead of a fun parody of disco, when the records exploded, a riot broke out on the field and the White Sox eventually forfeited the game. Anger was bubbling just beneath the surface, and the explosion of a few thousand disco records was all it took to unleash the beast on the baseball field. Little did any of us know that the decimation of disco was just the beginning of the changes we were about to experience as the eighties began. And it went deeper than Metallica replacing the Bee Gees on the Hot 100.

The following winter, another explosion took place on the ice rink of Lake Placid. When the US hockey team shocked the Soviet Union and the rest of the world and then went on to win the gold,[81] it seemed to mark the beginning of a time of optimism and hope for many Americans. At the end of the game against the Soviets, Al Michaels,[82] the famous announcer, asked us all if we believed in miracles and for just that one moment, I think we all did. But the economy was still shaky and many feared that newly elected President Reagan would do little to improve things. Changes were starting to spring up, but few would recognize them. Nobody believed their instincts anymore. We had all been wrong too many times in a row.

He who hesitates is lost, but sometimes not for long

After a decade of slumps, in August of 1982, it seemed like a gun went off. The great bull market of the eighties had begun, only nobody knew it. We were all programmed by then to expect the worst. I was new to the business and never really expected the market to move so fast. I wasn't alone. Ten years of a depressing market had fooled so many of us into believing that this was just another fake run that would eventually die out as so many previous rallies had done.

In hindsight it was so easy to see this was a dramatic turn. When you look at the period on a long-term stock chart—or for that matter, a chart on interest rates or inflation—the trend is as clear as day. Everything turned dramatically in August of 1982 while most of America was enjoying their end of summer vacation. Many claim they saw it, predicted it, and jumped on board fast while the getting was good, but the truth is, most folks were just on vacation.

One of the partners at the firm—I must give him credit—really felt that a bull market was on the way. I can still remember him coming into our investment meeting and insisting that this market movement was different, that this wasn't just a little trend—that big, significant change was coming. He then produced a list, I think it was on the back of an envelope with coffee stains on it, of the names of the classic growth stocks he thought would lead this new bull market: Proctor & Gamble, Bristol Myers, and Johnson & Johnson among others.

After a lengthy pause from Ken, our senior partner—he of the famous lengthy pauses—agreed, and our firm began a plan to plow money into the brand names on the back of that envelope. Ironically though, while these names would eventually lead the bull market of the eighties and make many investors like Peter Lynch[83] great names for themselves, they were not the names to lead in the early stages. That fell to the more risky, economically sensitive, cyclical companies. Missing much of this upside was frustrating as we were watching other firms make large gains, and some of our more aggressive clients started to get antsy. They felt like they were missing out on all the fun, but Ken held firm.

I was impressed with how he handled these conversations with frustrated clients. I have heard so many investment professionals blame outward or make excuses when things turn against them. It's the Fed, it's Congress, it's the president, it's company management. But Ken would shake his head and admit that we may have missed the boat this time. He would explain that we had wanted to stay with the safest, quality names and unfortunately these were not the names that were leading the market. We simply hadn't anticipated the explosion in cyclical stocks, and we were wrong. Perhaps we would have an opportunity to add to cyclical names in the future but at this point they were too high.

This approach worked, but even though our aggressive clients were sticking with us, as a result of my boss's transparency and good intentions, we felt the pressure internally. We waited and waited all through the end of 1983. By that time, another young associate and I were working directly with our research partner at the firm. He had told us that our first assignment was to study cyclical stocks to see how we might eventually jump in.

Every night my colleague and I would stay late, share ideas, and read research reports until eventually we began to narrow down the universe of cyclical companies to the ones we felt would do the best. We really felt, as very young associates at the firm, like we were finally making a difference. I had visions of sitting down with Louis Rukeyser on *Wall Street Week*,[84] the audience hanging on my every wise word. All this would be possible for me, I thought, just as soon as I saw a correction in cyclical stocks and could buy in at a reasonable price and make my mark. As 1983 ended, we had high hopes that a correction was close, and we were prepared with our stock picks.

Unfortunately, the market, as is typical, did not cooperate with our plans and instead took off like a rocket in the first few days of the New

Year. We kept thinking that it would back off, but it just kept pressing forward and ultimately most of the partners could take the pressure no longer. If 1984 was to be a repeat of 1983, we just could not sit idly by and watch our quality stocks do nothing while the market was making another run.

There was a big meeting that Wednesday afternoon. The research partner maintained that eventually it would pay off to wait and be patient. No one would hear of it. And then the company leadership learned that my colleague and I had been studying these cyclical stocks, and suddenly, all eyes turned to us. Our moment had arrived. It was decided that we should go home that night, pick our best stocks, and be ready to buy the next day.

It's hard to describe the excitement we felt. We were like kids in a candy store with an unlimited piggy bank. We felt like we'd finally hit the big time and got caught up in the headiness of the moment. We picked the riskiest and most aggressive stocks we could find, convinced that we could then make the firm, and of course ourselves, look like heroes. I picked steel and paper and no technology (I must have been listening to a lot of Springsteen back then). I think it's pretty obvious by now where this story is headed.

When we started buying the following morning, it was as if the market had anticipated our every move and carried these shares even higher. This made us look really smart and we took our bows, but the euphoria only lasted a few short hours. The very next day, the market began a substantial decline and did not recover for over a year. The cyclical stocks were hit the hardest. We no longer looked like geniuses. Some of our stocks declined 50% or more. Some, like my steel stock, never really recovered and sadly we hesitated to sell until much of the damage was done. It could have been the end of me.

Ironically, many of these cyclicals eventually rallied after the market bottomed later in the year, though they never dominated the market as they had in 1983. Indeed, it was the true growth stocks, including most of the stocks on the back of the partner's envelope, that began to lead the market.

Good investments have three good legs

Watching our favorite cyclical picks implode was a hard time for us as young associates. We felt the heat from the senior partners who had trusted us, and it was devastating watching our dreams of becoming stars on Wall Street crash and burn. Of course, as we were being blamed, it was easy to blame them right back. What were they thinking, asking the most junior of their firm to make such important decisions?

Thankfully, our next reaction was the one that probably saved our careers. We decided to treat this experience as our tuition at Stock Market University and learn from our mistakes. Here's what we learned: every stock has to have three legs, meaning that there are essentially three broad ways to look at a stock: Fundamentals, Valuation, and Technicals. Here's the rundown of those factors:

1. **Fundamentals.** The fundamentals refer to the story behind the stock, what the key products are, how the financials look, and what the long- and short-term growth prospects are for the company and their products.

2. **Valuation.** Valuation looks at how the company is valued in

the market. You arrive at a valuation by comparing a stock price to its earnings, sales, and book value. Then you compare that to the overall market, peers, and the company's own history.

3. **Technicals.** Technicals refer to the trend of the stock price over time, as often this picture can provide clues to future prices.

When my buddy and I went back and looked in detail at how we'd made our decisions on which stocks to buy, we realized that we had mostly focused on the fundamentals and essentially ignored the valuation and technicals. In addition, when evaluating fundamentals, we had a biased view because we had been disappointed by not owning these cyclicals stocks. We were all feeling pressure to get them into the firm's portfolio. So, when we evaluated potential growth, we were viewing things through an overly optimistic lens.

Additionally, we had completely ignored how these stocks were being valued in the market. By definition, cyclicals move up and down. When they are at all-time highs and expensive in relation to their earnings, an alarm bell should have gone off for us. But we didn't hear those alarms if they did sound because we were busy making emotional decisions.

Finally, regarding the technicals, we realized we had not even considered what the price trend was telling us. If we had, there would have been a warning that we were chasing the stocks we wanted to buy too far. Later, after the declines began, the charts could have warned us that some of these stocks had significantly further to fall, especially the steel stock that I had recommended, and would have caused us to fold up shop and cut our losses. We also realized that we had been in the grip of euphoria and unwilling to look at any warning signs.

The most important thing we learned was that through our new understanding of the mistakes we made, we had discovered how to make better decisions next time. As a result of our rocky start in the investment world, my colleague and I developed our own unique brand of analysis. We both became much more vocal with the senior partners from there on out because we had grown more confident and more secure in the fact that we had covered all our bases. We had earned our stripes, the hard way, and once you've tasted the agony of defeat and survived, you feel like you've earned the right to speak up.

Next, I convinced my bosses that since no one in our firm had a grasp of technical analysis, perhaps I could be the one to add that arrow to our quiver. I started to travel, talking with some of the top technicians in the world. I began participating in our investment meetings at a different level. I became more and more convinced over time that studying the technical trends was actually a study of the human emotions that ultimately drive the market. What I did not realize at the time but have discovered since is that the study of human emotions begins and ends with a better understanding yourself. This, I would eventually come to understand, was only the beginning of a life-long journey.

Throughout my career I have been thankful for the catastrophe of my steel stock. As opposed to ending my career, it helped to further my passion for the market and my genuine love for learning. I look back and think about my relationships in the same way. They are learning experiences that allow me to learn and grow, but only once I find the strength to face facts, become the master of my own impulses and emotions, and learn to let go.

The expression that no one rings a bell when the tide turns is surely true whether it be in the markets or in our personal lives. Whether it's an explosion of disco records or some great dispute, it is always a result of a compilation of many events. It is up to each of us to observe and decide whether a market move or a moment in a relationship is a decisive sea change or simply an adjustment in the current trend. We must take our time and then, usually with patience and observation, be able to see a clear trend emerge. We need to be careful that we're not so latched on to the old trend that we simply cannot make the shift to the new direction.

The Three-Legged Solution

1. **Fundamentals.** Learn the story behind the company. Know what the company's key products or services are, what their financial profile says, and what the possibilities are for growth both now, and long term. Note whether the stock tends to have long period of earnings growth or is more cyclical, as each will act differently over a long period of time and will help you decide whether the current trend in earnings and sales is long lasting or likely to give way.

2. **Valuation.** Analyze a stock's price to its earnings and revenues and then compare the valuation relative to its own history, to its competitors, and to the market as a whole.

3. **Technicals**. Evaluate the price trend of a stock. In addition, notice how these trends move relative to events in the company's earnings history as well as to events in the market

and in the economy. It is surprising how often prices move differently than how one might expect, and it is these trends that can give clues to future direction. I became enamored with studying technical trends and read everything I could find from modern day technicians to ones that had traded back in the early 1900s. I thought it fascinating that the same patterns that worked to help predict stock prices more than a hundred years ago still work in today's market. The technical trends of an asset will tell you a great deal, grounded in history, about what might be the future direction of prices.

One technician explained that while markets and companies may change, human emotions stay the same. Fear and hope, love and hate, desire and greed were as powerful a hundred years ago as they are today, and it's human emotion that drives the market, then and now. It turns out the market truly is like a Dostoevsky novel after all!

Inspiring Words You Can Take to the Bank

MONEY IS HUMAN

A man who has not passed through the inferno of his passions has never overcome them. As far as we can discern, the sole purpose of human existence is to kindle a light in the darkness of mere being. Everything that irritates us about others can lead us to an understanding of ourselves.[85]
—CARL JUNG

Patterns repeat, because human nature hasn't changed for thousands of years[86].
—EDWIN LEFÈVRE, *Reminiscences of a Stock Operator,* 1923

Be careful what you water your dreams with. Water them with worry and fear and you will produce weeds that choke the life from your dream. Water them with optimism and solutions and you will cultivate success. Always be on the lookout for ways to turn a problem into an opportunity for success. Always be on the lookout for ways to nurture your dream.[87]
—LAO TZU

CHAPTER 7

YOUR GREATEST FEARS CAN BE YOUR BEST FRIENDS IN DISGUISE

The Art of the Unknown

I am a pretty mellow guy for the most part and I like it that way. I work at keeping things on an even keel. I guess I've gotten pretty good at it by now, because people are known to ask me, "Mick, don't you ever blow your stack?" If my son happens to be nearby, he'll jump in with both feet and tell the infamous tale of the day his dad went postal at Auckland Airport in New Zealand.

We had taken a vacation to visit my older son, who was doing an internship in New Zealand for the summer. It had been a beautiful visit, taking in majestic ocean views and enjoying our resort in the middle of a lush forest (notice I said resort, not camping site!). We had even gone boogie boarding down massive sand dunes, which my daughter keeps reminding me is called sand boarding, not boogie boarding. To tie everything up with a bow, the trip home was going to include a stop in Maui, one of my favorite places in the world.

We were all blissing out, only a plane ride away from our next island paradise… and then we got to the airport. The trouble started at check-in. We were told that our plane had turned out to be a smaller aircraft than they expected, and they couldn't fit all of us on board. As a result, they began randomly rebooking some of us onto different flights. I watched my island bliss-bubble pop right there in the terminal.

They did give us some choice in the matter, however. We could either fly to Los Angeles and then catch another fight to Maui, which was way out of the way and a crazy travel time to get to Maui, or we could wait two days and fly to Maui direct. These didn't sound like choices at all. The only real alternative was to head directly to Los Angeles, then home to San Diego and skip the trip to Maui. When I realized this, I, the unflappable Mick Heyman, completely lost it.

Now, I do understand that these are first-world problems, but in the moment, it felt like a cruel twist of fate. I was like, What? Why our seats? Are you kidding me? I was furious—outraged. Someone had stolen my island paradise. Luckily, I had my kids with me, so I kept it clean and did not wind up in the Auckland city jail. I did, however, express my displeasure to every poor unsuspecting gate attendant on duty that day.

Of course, you cannot fight the airlines. You will never win. It's like trying to fight weather. And they had handled far more terrifying anger balls than me. I didn't stand a chance. They eventually appeased us with a little money and a few drinks, and I consoled myself with memories of a wonderful trip with my kids down under, no jail time, and the fact that I was heading home to where I lived very happily in one of the most beautiful places in the world. I remembered that I was a lucky man and made peace with letting the Maui trip pass on by. The flight back was bumpy, and suddenly, I couldn't wait to get home. Maybe it had all been for the best.

When we finally landed in Los Angeles, I saw that my son in New Zealand had texted, telling us to check the news. He'd punctuated his message with one of those upside-down crazy smiley emojis, so I knew something big was up. My other son checked and saw that Hawaii was getting hit with a Category 5 hurricane, one of the largest in recent memory. Our five days in Maui would have been spent staring out the window watching wind and rain—and that was the best-case scenario. My son couldn't stop laughing.

"Nice job, Dad," he kept saying, shaking with laughter he couldn't suppress. "You really pulled it out of the fire this time."

Inspiring Words You Can Take to the Bank

BACK TO THE FUTURE

It's tough to make predictions, especially about the future.[88]
—YOGI BERRA (AS ATTRIBUTED BY RANDALL FOSKEY)

Man suffers only because he takes seriously what the Gods made for fun[89]
—ALAN WATTS

Life is a series of natural and spontaneous changes. Don't resist them; don't wish things were different. That only creates sorrow. Go along. Let reality be reality. Let things flow naturally forward in whatever way they like. Be like a pebble carried effortlessly along the stream of life. [90]
—VERNON HOWARD *(explaining Taoism)*

Don't get married to your expectations for the future

My son's laughter was justified.

I was asking for it that day. I was doing something I rarely do by refusing to roll with the punches. I ignored everything I've learned from a lifetime of mellow money management, and all because the airlines had shattered my expectations. I wasn't satisfied with New Zealand, or seeing my son, or sweeping oceanscapes, or lush forest resorts. I wanted more and more and better and right away, because that's what I'd been banking on.

Fortunately, I never did get to have my cake and eat it too, because if I had, I would have wound up staring out the window at a soggy beach, cursing the weather and my wretched misfortune for stranding me on an island in the middle of a Cat 5 hurricane. And who knows how long it would have taken me to get back to my beautiful and beloved home!

None of us can know what the future holds or how events will eventually total out in the end. Often, when we think we are acting in our own best interests, it turns out to be just the opposite.

Life and the market require a little faith that things will work out as long as we act responsibly and with good intentions.

I should have known this long before I ever threw that fit in Auckland. After all, I had learned that lesson many years before when I made the decision to move down to Dixieland.

Me and my kids enjoying a waterfall and some sand boarding in New Zealand

Boredom is life's way of telling you to invite a little risk

I was nervous about moving down south for many reasons. I had a lot of preconceptions about the south, impressions I probably picked up while watching the *Beverly Hillbillies* growing up. When the call came in from my friend Paul to join his company down there, I felt like I was going to wind up in a shotgun shack in a holler with a neighbor named Jethro. I didn't reason with myself that it was only just across the Ohio River from me, a mere hundred or so miles from Cincinnati, where I lived. Sometimes, inches can seem like miles.

Despite my reservations, a change sounded good to me. My wife, Hong, was Chinese. We were a bit of an odd couple—a scientist from China and an investment counselor from Dayton, Ohio. Where we lived you didn't see that combo very often. The only Chinese person I had ever met before I met my wife was the waitress at my local Chinese restaurant. So, while I wasn't sure how Jethro and Elly May were going to feel about us, at least down there we would stand out together.

I met my wife at a party at the home of a mutual friend. I first spied her by the spinach dip and remembered I'd seen her selling hotdogs at the ballpark the week before. I asked for her number, memorized it when I didn't have a pen, and then figured if I remembered her number, it was meant to be. If I forgot, well, then it wasn't. It was a 50/50 shot, and I was prepared to accept either result. Ah, youth.

Of course, I remembered her number, called her the next day, and before I knew it, we were in love. This is a testament to the wonderful things that can happen when you leave yourself open to unexpected developments. From the moment Hong and I met, everything just flowed so naturally and easily. Sometimes cultural differences would pop up, but we just thought it was funny and moved on. One birthday I gave her a watch. She told me later that in China, when you give somebody a watch for their birthday, you are kind of saying you wish they never see another birthday. We laughed about it then, but I never made that mistake again!

Hong and I just rolled with it together pretty much from the moment we met. We survived the hiccups, and as time went by, our love grew strong. As opposed to my first marriage which felt like one forced decision after another, this relationship seemed to just flow.

It was obvious we should get married, and so we did, and began our family in the same relaxed, inevitable style.

On the job front, I was starting to get fed up with the bank where I was now working. All the decisions had been taken out of my hands and centralized into a committee, where I did not have a seat at the table. There was going to be no room for my creativity or for customizing portfolios for my clients based on their unique goals. It was a steady paycheck, and the work wasn't hard, but it was not in sync with my passion for managing money.

I started tossing around the idea of leaving the bank, hanging out a shingle, and launching the Mick Heyman Investment Firm. I thought that had a real ring to it. It looked like the obvious next step, and I felt confident that my loyal clients would follow me. Then, out of the blue, my friend Paul called me from Louisville, Kentucky, and another wave rose out of the ocean.

Now, I had a decision to make. Would I go out on my own and incur the risks of entrepreneurialism? Or would I take the safer bet and take another job, even though the location was not ideal? It was Hong, the more adventurous one of us, who made the final decision.

"I certainly didn't come all the way to America to wind up in Kentucky of all places," she said. "But why not try it for a few years? We can always move if we don't like it. Your clients will follow you wherever and whenever you decide to go." Hong was right. I wasn't risking anything but a little time, and we still had plenty of that. So, I called Paul, told him I'd take the job, and we packed up the wagon and moved on down to Dixie.

The company was called National Asset Management.[91] Paul had high hopes for it. He wanted to put them on the map, and he wanted me to help him do that. It sounded good, but secretly I thought to myself, Me? In Louisville, Kentucky? I was surely skeptical but fate, however, knew better than I did, and the joke, once again, was on me.

The company managed money for institutions, such as endowments, corporations, and union plans. They had outperformed the S&P 500 for three straight years and since the institutional business is highly performance sensitive relative to beating the S&P 500, they had really been on a roll and their client list was growing as a result.

Paul said I would be a perfect fit given my investment experience. He thought that I could add value with my investment insight and my ability to take care of existing clients. He also thought I could be helpful on the marketing end since they were overwhelmed with requests for presentations for new clients. There was a lot of buzz based on their stellar returns and they needed to turn that buzz into bottom line results.

I was excited about this new opportunity, despite the regional ramifications. The new company would allow me to continue managing money for my existing clients, so I wasn't giving up old relationships. And I would be forming new relationships, with new and bigger clients, who I hadn't worked with before. Institutions wanted to see performance in the short term, and they hired consultants to analyze this performance and make recommendations to hire and fire managers. Large committees would evaluate how we were doing on a quarterly basis. In a way, I felt like I was stepping into a larger arena. And of course, the money they were offering didn't hurt either. More money almost never hurts.

FROM BOTH SIDES NOW

The Beverly Hillbillies (1993)[92]

DIRECTOR: *Penelope Spheeris*

STARS: *Lily Tomlin, Cloris Leachman, Dolly Parton, Jim Varney*

This is a movie remake of the classic TV series from 1962 featuring a hillbilly from the Deep South who strikes oil and moves his family on up to Beverly Hills, where they recreate the Ozarks[93] in the heart of movieland. It's a great reminder that no matter where you go, there you are, and how our misguided regional prejudices fade away once it moves right next door.

Deliverance (1972)[94]

DIRECTOR: *John Boorman*

STARS: *John Voigt, Burt Reynolds, Ned Beatty*

This movie is a terrifying metaphor for man's inhumanity to nature, and man's inhumanity to man. Do not watch this one before going river rafting in the back woods. You will sleep with one eye open.

Scent of a Woman (1992)[95]

DIRECTOR: *John Brest*

STARS: *Al Pacino, Chris O'Donnell*

A beautifully acted story exploring the themes of conscience and the human spirit that seeks to improve one's condition despite feeling despondent and hopeless. We all can benefit from learning to follow our true path, despite the struggles we may encounter. Al Pacino's speech at the end is both inspiring and hilarious at the same time, perhaps the greatest movie speech I've ever heard.

When you bury your fears, they grow

Once I got settled in Louisville, things started to get real. Pretty soon I realized that the situation was not quite as I had imagined it. First of all, it became clear that, at that point, the company didn't need my investment experience. What they really wanted was for me to make as many presentations in as short a time as possible and turn the leads into new business. This was not good news, because I feared public speaking and was surely not confident in my abilities.

I was great one on one. I was very used to talking with people, listening proactively, learning about their hopes and fears, and then describing how we would meet their objectives in the long run. This is a very different animal than making presentations to large committees, while still coming off as my authentic, humble, likable, nice-guy-even-in-a-shit-storm self.

The fact of the matter was, I was not good at making presentations in front of large groups. My voice was too soft, and my personality seemed to disappear. I hated and feared public speaking. And I knew I wasn't alone. I once heard that when asked what their greatest fear was, most Americans polled listed public speaking as #1 with death coming in second. I concurred with most Americans. Full stop.

I was essentially born with stage fright. Communication was a hurdle for me from the beginning. My parents put me in speech therapy early on because I had trouble pronouncing certain letters. For a good stretch of time, my mom was the only one who could make out a word I said. The only time I was able to express myself clearly to others without my mom translating was when I didn't like my food. On that score, apparently, I was able to make myself quite clear.

Thankfully, speech therapy helped me to express myself so that the world could understand. I can still remember the excitement of being able to finally pronounce my best friend's name correctly for the very first time. Unfortunately, this experience left me feeling insecure about my speaking abilities, and it had plagued me ever since. Four years of college and I can't remember raising my hand once. In time, with the help of those who loved me, and a Dale Carnegie class or two,[96] I was comfortable enough to be myself in front of a group. But that certainly didn't nominate me as the guy most likely to succeed as a public speaker. And now here I was, in a job that had me headed for center stage. All my old fears returned.

It certainly ignited a bit of a personal crisis for me. This was a high-powered firm and I wanted to succeed. Yet here I was, facing down an old demon from my childhood that was standing right in the middle of my path to achievement. I decided I had no choice but to turn around and face the fear head on.

To begin with, I reached out to the music department at the University of Louisville thinking that as much as I hated singing (I took after my mom in talent), perhaps facing this fear and learning how to get my voice to carry would help me feel stronger vocally, and therefore be more confident on stage. The music department referred me to the theater department, which was lucky for me and anyone else within ear shot. Also lucky for me, I met Trudy, a theater professor, who was willing to work with me once a week on voice projection and learning how to relax and be myself in front of a crowd.

Right away, Trudy put me on camera and asked me to describe a scary experience, like the time I climbed that stupid rock in Baja and got stuck at the top. Then she asked me to explain how I managed stocks. Then she played the tape back to me and asked, "Who would you hire, the funny rock-climber guy or the guy boring you with his stock picking description?" Can you guess who won? The message was clear. I will always remember her number one rule, which she repeated to me at every opportunity. "Mick," she would say, looking me dead in the eyes to make sure she was connecting, "Mick, do not act. Ever. You are not an actor! But as yourself, you are likable and believable. So, don't act, Mick. Don't ever act. Just be yourself."

A few months later, the firm decided to have a practice session on giving presentations and when I had my chance, I noticed people exchange curious looks, wondering what they were about to see. I think that folks were frightened for me. I had been a little cringeworthy in the past, and I knew it. After a few moments, though, the curious looks turned to shocked expressions as my voice carried strongly, and I looked quite comfortable giving the talk. I soon found I was being successful at winning new business and, more surprisingly, having fun doing it. I found it ironic but illuminating that one of my biggest fears growing up had just become one of my greatest strengths and all because I had learned to face my fears and remembered to never, ever try to be an actor.

From meeting Hong, to taking the job in Louisville to finding success in public speaking, the directions my life have taken have been unpredictable. Learning how to be open to whatever new twists and turns my path presented has been one of the most important lessons I've learned about living a happy life and having a successful investment style. Our crystal balls on what the future holds are fuzzy at best. Whether it's a plane cancelation or a job opportunity or meeting a girl at a party, it's hard to predict how and where our paths will lead. Along the way I have always been helped when I have kept an open mind, and when I don't, fate usually gives me a strong reminder that control in life is fleeting.

As in life, so it is in the marketplace. We all wish for a consistent, predictable return that we can count on. But from what I have learned from Buddhism, it is in our desires that we find misery and suffering. If we can be open to the unpredictability in the markets, I have found that decisions are less chaotic and less prone to panic, which usually only results in better returns over the long haul.

When we look back through history, it's easy to see that random events and choices seem to fit together like a puzzle, that market returns year to year fit quite well with seemingly random events. It's only in the moment, when we're in the thick of it, that things seem arbitrary and out of control. Breathe, stay open, and enjoy every moment, because you only get one ride on the roller coaster. Make it a joyful one that isn't bound in by fear or expectations.

Tips for Tongue-Tied Public Speakers

1. **Do things from time to time that make you uncomfortable.** Placing yourself in situations that are unfamiliar to you helps you learn how to relax and roll with unexpected changes in plans.

2. **Take a theater course, take a singing lesson.** Stepping out of your box and doing something that you know you aren't good at or are embarrassed to do will make you immune to future embarrassment and help you to realize that embarrassment will not kill you but make you stronger.

3. **Practice speaking in front of a camera, and then watch yourself back.** I know this can be painful at first, but it will help you to understand when you are engaging, when you are boring, when you look awkward, and when you flow.

4. **Engage an audience of people close to you, who won't judge, and practice a speech or presentation in front of them.** Ask for their feedback, make adjustments, and then try it again. The only road to Carnegie Hall is through practice, practice, practice.

5. **The things we most fear in life can turn out to be our greatest strengths.** So don't assume that just because you are afraid of public speaking you are necessarily bad at it.

LEARNING FROM YOUR WINS AND YOUR LOSSES

Even More Special When You Can Share with Teammates and Loved Ones

Recently my son and I were out on the golf course, which is something we've done together since he and his brother were little. Since my son hadn't played golf in a while, we decided to play a scramble or what's known as a "best ball game,"[97] and just relax. In a best ball game, you play as a team. Each player hits the ball from the same spot, and the best ball gets the score for the team, so if one of us hits a good shot, we are rooting for each other. We had played a scramble the day before and had scored even par as a team, so today we were hoping to improve on that.

As we were about to tee off, a family pulled up in their cart and asked to play with us. The father and son were golfing, and Mom had come along for the ride. We agreed to it, but they decided they would rather compete with each other than join our game of best ball. Immediately, there was a clear difference in their dialogue versus ours, which Mom noticed with some awkwardness. Their swords were drawn, and Dad and son were locked in a battle of some kind that had nothing to do with golf. I recognized this type of father and son dynamic instantly, between the generation that has something to prove and the older one that is holding on. I had experienced this friction myself once, and I didn't miss the heat, not one bit.

On a much hotter day than that one, many, many years ago when I was around 15 or 16, I had taken on my dad in much the same way. We had just arrived in Palm Springs. We were on vacation as a family, and my dad told me that as soon as we got to the hotel, we were going to play tennis. I knew what that meant: a grueling battle with rackets in our hands.

I had imagined this vacation to be about swimming in the hotel pool and looking for girls. Instead, we were going to play a game of tennis in 110-degree heat. I could hardly breathe just walking from the car to the room. And to make matters worse, on the way to the tennis court we had to walk past the swimming pool where my sisters were laughing and playing, all cooled off from the car ride and having the time of their lives. I looked toward the tennis court with a thousand-mile stare.

My dad and I played frequently, and I had only started beating him within the last year. Dad was a competitive guy who had been taught to win and saw the lessons in overcoming adversity. But I was blind to the larger lesson, in the way that teenagers usually are. I only saw the battle. And although I was beginning to get the edge, the results of those wins never felt victorious. In the end it wasn't winning that was going to make me feel better, it was growing up, and that was not going to happen in one tennis match, or even 20. Nonetheless, that didn't stop me from trying to beat him. Hence, every time we hit the court it felt like a cage fight.

Growing up, my dad seemed like a giant to me. He was a renowned lawyer and a respected leader in our community. Wherever we went, we would hear stories from clients, friends, and family who had benefited from his insight and willingness to go the extra mile for them.

He worked long hours and came home exhausted and looking to cool down. Unfortunately, we kids often only saw the exhaustion. We didn't understand what he was going through or that he was working to help his clients in need. All we knew was that Dad was always tired when he got home. Then he'd get frustrated that his kids seemed more interested in *Gilligan's Island* than greeting him when he walked through the door. It was a total disconnect that I would not understand until many years later.

My dad could be formidable, but to his credit, he was always there when we needed support. Once, I was in a car accident that was my fault, having waited too long to slow down on a rainy day and I rear-ended a lady. I remember the fear of calling Dad and telling him that it was my fault, but his reaction was, "Thank God you are okay, that is all that matters." Later that evening the lady called us up during dinner. She wanted to let my dad know that her neck hurt because of his son. Dad told her to take a couple of aspirin and that she'd better think twice about threatening his son. He came back to the dinner table, a half-smile on his face—that night we smiled with him.

It wasn't always a battle, either. My dad is the one who taught me to swim and to love the ocean. We both felt the joy of body surfing from when I was three and enjoy it together even today as he turns 91. Why are my kids so in love with the ocean? It passed on naturally to them through the generations.

My most exciting sports memory with him was standing together in Riverfront Stadium[98] as Johnny Bench hit a shocking home run over the right field wall in the '72 baseball playoffs,[99] setting the stage for one of the greatest comebacks in Reds' history. I can still remember my dad standing on the seat next to me, pure joy on both our faces, cheering for the home team.

We had much to celebrate in those years and yet, it's hard for a boy to grow up if he can't eventually compare favorably with his dad, and every once in a while win the contest. Back then it seemed only through competition that a son could finally earn his dad's respect.

Such were the milestone issues on the line that day on the tennis court. My dad was playing well. Although I was hell bent on winning, my dad was running my shots down and continuing to hold serve. At some point the match was tied. We were both red-faced and exhausted. The smart thing to do would have been to call it a draw and get off the court and into the damn pool already. But we weren't thinking about that. We were locked in on each other, and although I could still hear my sisters in the pool, shrieking with delight, I was not going to give in.

Winning isn't everything and is certainly not the only thing

I made a strategic decision at that point to keep returning the ball, because I knew that time and endurance were on my side. Of course, he couldn't run down every shot, though he surely tried. In the end, I won but I did not feel victorious. Ten years later, sitting on a couch and talking with a therapist, I was still going back over this titanic battle with my father. Many of the dilemmas I was encountering in my adult relationships all seemed to come back to my dad and the hollow victories of my youth, much like that one. "It's all about your dad," the therapist would say over and over, and he was right. But it was also about the nature of the competition between us, a rivalry between fathers and sons that was ubiquitous in our culture at the time.

I watched myself repeat these battles in my relationships at home, at work with my bosses, and ultimately, with my investment decisions in the stock market. Trust me, the last thing you want to do as an investor is to try and prove your worth and metaphorically beat your dad by trying to beat the stock market at its own game. Try it, and you will eventually lose: though the market may tease you, let you think you are on top of the world, let you shine in front of your friends and loved ones, in the end it will catch up to you. Ego is an investor's Achilles heel.

It wasn't until many years later that I really won that match with my dad. And I didn't win by running him down on the courts as I did back in Palm Springs. I won by explaining to him, in a loving way, how much I had been afraid of him when I was young, how I felt so small relative to the giant I saw him to be. I explained that I often felt that

I wasn't good enough growing up, even when I managed to win. Not surprisingly, he remembered our match from that day too.

At first, my dad reminded me of all the good things in my childhood, all the blessings he had bestowed upon me, all of which I acknowledged to be true. But in the end, he also listened and appreciated my need to talk about some of the pain I had felt, and as we talked it was clear he understood me. He let me know that he loved me, and that he was proud of me.

That was the day that my dad and I both experienced an awakening, both in ourselves and in our relationship. He could finally see me as an equal, and I could see him as a loving father. We were at last able to joke together about that crazy tennis match on that sweltering day long ago that nearly killed us both.

As we were leaving that day, I mentioned how I had loved spending time with his parents when they were alive, but how, no matter what, my grandfather (his dad) never let me get close to winning at checkers, even when I was little. Dad smiled wistfully and said, "He never let me win either."

My son and I did break par that day and we were excited when we did it. When we play, occasionally I will hit a freak of nature drive and be almost up to where one of my son's balls are and I will be pretty excited about that too, and my son will be happy for me. Competition is a natural part of life, and we naturally feel good when we rise up to our best—and I'll admit it, when our best means we win, that is fun too!

So, there is no natural conclusion of whether competition is good or bad—it's more about awareness. This is what eventually helped me to talk through things with my dad, and that, in itself, brought great meaning to my life. Certainly, competition can bring out the best in us, but it can also bring outcomes we don't anticipate—or want. Teamwork, however, always inspires a sense of togetherness and joy in accomplishment. Victories are more fulfilling when they are shared.

Me and my dad sharing our passion for the ocean

Inspiring Words You Can Take to the Bank

66

INVESTOR KNOW THYSELF

If you don't know who you are, then the stock market is an expensive way to find out.[100]
—EDWIN LEFÈVRE, *Reminiscences of a Stock Operator,* 1923

Let's not forget that the little emotions are the great captains of our lives and we obey them without realizing it.[101]
—VINCENT VAN GOGH

Dream lofty dreams, and as you dream, so you shall become.[102]
—JAMES ALLEN

The spirit of competition can be a double-edged sword

Years ago in the market, competition was a blood sport. Money, the way it was earned, handled, lost, and made back was the stuff of legend. Movies like *Wall Street* or *Bonfire of the Vanities* gave us trader antiheroes who were macho, ruthless, and rich beyond measure—and almost always men. They were married to gorgeous women, had opulent homes, and drove fierce cars. They were outlaws straight out of the Wild West in Paul Stuart suits.[103] Jesse James with a penthouse and a private jet. Today these heroes are of any gender, but the style has not changed much.

My company in Louisville was a far cry from Wall Street, but even Dixieland wasn't immune to the testosterone-fueled spirit of competition. We had our own drama, and while it couldn't stack up to the opulence of Wall Street in the go-go nineties, it felt just as real and emotional to us. Although the firm had been on a good roll before I came on board, the year I joined it underperformed the market for the first time in three years. No one worried about it too much in the beginning, and the team managing the stocks seemed confident that 1994 would be better. As the year unfolded, however, and while I was focusing on polishing my presentation skills, stock performance continued to stutter.

In the institutional business, two years of underperformance is nigh on catastrophic. Institutions tend to focus on quarter-to-quarter performance, so this period of underperformance was raising some alarms. Most clients were forgiving because of the previous run of good performance, but patience was wearing thin and as we entered 1995, we worried that the firm could topple if things didn't improve.

Decision-making was scrutinized more and more closely. It seemed that there was a lot of dysfunction and poor communication in the group that was picking the stocks. It wasn't that the stock picks were all disappointing. but no one on the team was really analyzing the top-down aspect of how the portfolio stacked up in terms of cyclicality. This top-down view would have helped to mitigate much of the underperformance, but they weren't functioning with a holistic perspective. They weren't working like they were part of a team.

At that point, leadership decided to switch up the stock team and put somebody on with added experience, but also enough humility to air in without dominating the group. Leadership asked me to step in. They thought that I had knowledge and willingness to share without disrupting the existing culture of the group. I said I'd give it a try.

Inspiring Words You Can Take to the Bank

66

If you want to lift yourself up, lift up someone else.[104]
—BOOKER T. WASHINGTON

If you want to go fast, go alone. If you want to go far, go together.[105]
—AFRICAN PROVERB

It is the long history of humankind (and animal kind, too) that those who learned to collaborate and improvise most effectively have prevailed.[106]
—CHARLES DARWIN

In basketball—as in life—true joy comes from being fully present in each and every moment, not just when things are going your way.[107]
—PHIL JACKSON, *former Los Angeles Lakers and Chicago Bulls head coach*

On a championship team, even the star players are team players

Unfortunately, by the time I stepped into the group, I wasn't joining a real team at all. At that point it was every man for himself, which just typified the culture at the time, and in addition, no one on the team was happy to have another person—namely me—step in and infringe on what little autonomy they had left. It was a frustrating time.

Eventually, not only was the stock management team apparently dysfunctional, but then there was a struggle for power on the firm management team. This could have resulted in the firm collapsing as no institution wants to keep their money in a firm that had seen results slipping and was now coping with turmoil at the top levels of management. It was a curious struggle filled with what I felt were silly accusations but could have caused so much harm and was seemingly a fight for control of what, at the time, was a faltering investment firm in Louisville, Kentucky. When I look back, it appeared all this controversy was born from a competitive streak that just couldn't resist winning at any cost.

Most of us grow up and out of the overwhelming need to beat our competitors into the dust, even if those competitors are our own teammates. And when you don't, you may hold power for a while, but eventually there is always someone out to get you. Eventually, the firm, led by my friend Paul, joined together and demanded that this culture of competition be put to an end. As a result, in place of competition, we structured the firm like a team playing best ball golf, where every success is celebrated by the team, and every failure is jointly held.

I was excited to be in on this effort. This was a chance to see if better organizational structure and healthy teamwork could improve results. We thought that combining all of our unique talents into a group effort gave us the best chance of success. What happened next would dramatically change the direction of the company and demonstrate the power of cooperation and humility.

Jealousy and competition had so threatened the company that we decided to begin anew by evening out the playing field in stock management. Everyone on the stock team would be rewarded the same no matter what their assignment was, no matter what their individual stock picks had done. We were resolved. No stars. Our goal was now to outperform the market and other firms, not compete among ourselves.

Some of us were more involved in marketing, some with client service, some were purely looking at stocks. Some might be more fortunate with their stock picks some years, others might recommend a few losers, but it wouldn't matter—all was equal. In fact, we never told anyone outside the group who had recommended a stock, and in this way, every recommendation became a team recommendation, not an individual one. Our company would have no scapegoats and no standout celebrities.

Whenever a consultant came in to evaluate us, they always asked, who is the star? Who is the main stock picker? They were convinced that there had to be one shining intellect behind our process, because that's how the industry was typically run. We hear of Peter Lynch or Warren Buffet or John Templeton, not their teams. We never flinched. We always said our picks were made by the team. And in 1995, we began a year of stellar out-performance of the S&P 500 that would last for six consecutive years. In the end, our equity performance rose to the top decile of all institutional money managers, and large companies like Invesco wanted to acquire our expertise. Eventually, they did. I always attribute our success in those years to the humility of the group and to Paul, who put the firm first and kept it on a solid footing by using competition to our advantage and focusing on a team approach that allowed our own competitive instincts to work together. We played best ball.

Competition is not necessarily a bad thing. It can obviously help us all to raise the bar and up our game. But humility always needs to be part of the rules of play. We should never put our self-worth on the line, in any game, or with any investment choice. When we pick a stock, whether for ourselves or for a client, on our own or as part of a team, it is best if we do so because we think that stock can perform well, not just prove how smart or visionary we are.

With humility we can admit that the future is unpredictable, that sometimes things will go our way in the stock market and sometimes they won't. We can absorb surprises when they happen, not take it personally, and respond with strategy rather than a bruised ego. We should invest to make money over a period of time, not to prove we can overcome anxieties from childhood that have extended into adulthood.

Ironically, my dad and I became quite a team at managing his own assets. He has his own unique style combining a long-term view of stocks with an aggressiveness to hold on to long-term winners despite, at times, oversized positions. But instead of competing with our styles, we chose to blend his more aggressive style with my more conservative one.

We have enjoyed enormous success with this approach over the years—managing money together has brought us closer. It has taught us life lessons about how to compromise and mix our own temperaments, to blend competition with humility to gain success in our lives and in our net worth.

Rules for balancing competitive instincts and focusing them on winning the long game:

1. **Don't work out your childhood trauma in the marketplace.** Leave it in the therapist's office where it belongs.

2. **Don't avoid your issues.** When you bury them, they only grow, and eventually impact your wealth, both emotionally and financially.

3. **Competition is natural and positive, but not when the need to win eclipses your better judgment or your relationships.** Winning has its place. So does losing. Learn to grow from both experiences.

4. **When investing in the markets, we need to be aware that we are investing in the future, not trying to prove how smart we are.** The market will eventually provide you with its verdict and likely we will be exactly as good at overcoming unpredictable events in the market as we are at adapting to unforeseen events and overcoming adversity in our lives. Be good at both.

CHAPTER 9

THE MARKET IS COUNTERINTUITIVE

The Crazy Mixed-Up Rules of Investment in Bizarro World

Every month or so when I was young, my parents would put us in the car, and we'd go to visit both of their families. They all lived in roughly the same area in Cincinnati, and both families were incredibly sweet. We went to my mom's parents' house every year for Christmas and even though we are Jewish, Santa Claus would reliably climb down the chimney with presents for all of us. My grandparents believed in having their cake and eating it too, and they saw no reason that being Jewish should preclude us from getting Christmas presents as well as Hannukah presents. It was the best of both worlds.

My cousins would often join us for games, especially in the summertime. We'd play what was affectionately called ghost in the graveyard, which as far as I could tell was just an old-fashioned name for hide and seek, but this version sounded much more dangerous and exciting. When we visited my dad's folks, we would be treated to walks in the park or a game of checkers. Grandpa would kick my butt, but I didn't care. I just enjoyed spending time, even just sitting and watching TV with him while the delicious smell of my grandma's German cooking mingled with the tobacco in my grandpa's pipe.

My wise and wonderful grandparents

Among all of these sweet memories, though, there is one that still fills me with dread. And that is the memory of my indomitable Uncle Lew. Inevitably, as we kids were playing in the den or watching TV, the doorbell would ring. The happy activity and conversation and laughter would cease. We would freeze. Grandpa would get up and make his way slowly to the door. Then we'd hear Lew's telltale voice booming in the entry way. "Where's my boy?" he'd holler as soon as his foot crossed the threshold. "Where is he? Can't hide from me!"

Oh no, I would think with my stomach in knots. *It's Uncle Lew!* I would hesitate, desperately searching for a place to hide or ideally, hoping to disappear into thin air, but I knew there was no escape, so I'd have to get up and go say hello. Uncle Lew would grab me by the ears, put me in a headlock, and rap his knuckles against my skull. "Say uncle!" he'd bellow, giving me merciless noogies along with his predictable pun, and he wouldn't stop until I surrendered. "Come on, kid, say it. Say uncle!"

This is not an uncommon experience for boys of my age at that time. It was the male version of your aunt pinching your cheeks too hard. I don't know what this friendly sadism was designed to teach us youngsters. Maybe it was supposed to toughen us up or something. Perhaps Lew's rough and tumble greeting was designed to get me ready for the full contact sport of adult life. Only, in Lew's game, there weren't any referees to call a personal foul.

The grownups in the room would just smile, shake their heads, probably thinking, *that's crazy Uncle Lew!* and then go back to their bridge hand. So eventually, I had to say uncle. What other choice did I have? But I didn't like it. Thankfully as the years went by, there was always a younger brother or cousin to replace us older kids as the victims of Lew's affection. Apparently, growing up was the only defense against it.

The memory of Uncle Lew's noogies and crying uncle came back vividly to me on October 19, 1987—Black Monday as it is now known—when the market dropped about 22% in a single day. That dreadful afternoon left me with a feeling of absolute panic in the pit of my stomach, just like when I'd hear Uncle Lew coming through the door bellowing, "Where's my boy?" And once again, I felt like crying uncle.

The market had been going down all the previous week, and our firm had talked about the fact that it was looking vulnerable. When the roller coaster hit the apex and hurtled straight downhill, vulnerable wasn't the word we were using anymore.

"What the hell is happening? This is a full-on shit-show!" my boss Ken, who did not normally swear, roared from his corner office.

Despite the sheer terror we all felt in that moment, Ken told us there was nothing we could do. So, while our stock prices plummeted through the floor, we had to just sit there and stare at our monitors.

Finally, unable to handle doing nothing while the world ended, one of the partners started selling off one of the electric utilities we owned.

"What a joke," Ken groused. "Talk about rearranging deck chairs on the Titanic." He's crying uncle I thought, and that's how I was feeling too. I felt helpless in the grip of a force larger than myself, unable to resist or stop the pain. I wanted to do something, but there was nothing to do but sell, and selling felt like surrender. Selling felt like crying uncle, and something in me, maybe something my Uncle Lew managed to teach me after all, just wouldn't let me do that.

TOM HANKS REMINDS YOU TO NEVER, NEVER, NEVER GIVE UP

Forrest Gump (1994)

DIRECTOR: *Robert Zemeckis*

STARS: *Tom Hanks, Robin Wright, Gary Sinise, Sally Fields*

Forrest Gump, with braces on his legs and an IQ of 75, learns to not only walk but to run. And through pure luck, runs through most of the landmark moments in history, impacting the world without even meaning to. Forrest Gump reminds us that the only limits are the ones we place on ourselves.

The DaVinci Code (2006)

DIRECTOR: *Ron Howard*

STARS: *Tom Hanks, Ian McKellen, Alfred Molina, Audrey Tautou*

If a symbologist can solve a 2,000-year-old mystery by interpreting the clues in DaVinci's paintings, you can do anything. This is a great reminder that if you stick with it long enough, you really can find the holy grail.

Cast Away (2000)

DIRECTOR: *Robert Zemeckis*

STARS: *Tom Hanks, Helen Hunt*

A FedEx executive crash lands on a desert island and must endure years of isolation and hunger until he at last is rescued. Tom Hanks gives us a great reminder to never, never, never give up, even if your only friend is a soccer ball named Wilson.

Sometimes it takes more strength to do nothing than to do something

The day after Black Monday, we all trudged back into work ready for another day in the fallout shelter. I along with a few of the other partners realized that Ken had been right about doing nothing, and we thanked him for not giving in to the panic. In a market free fall, that feeling of just wanting to do something, anything, to make the pain go away drives you to do the opposite of what you really should be doing in a moment like that. Thankfully, with Ken's help, we had resisted that urge. And then, since prices were now so low, rather than selling, we began to buy.

This was the first time that I associated that "cry uncle" lesson of Uncle Lew's with market bottoms. Since then, it's become a feeling that I rely on, and I've realized it's a valuable feeling because it signals opportunity.

You can't trust your instincts until you can interpret what they are telling you

We all want to feel good and certain when we step into an investment. Oddly enough though, it's the times when we feel the worst that we can reap the greatest value.

My boss used to say that it never feels good when the time is best to make money. So before you can take advantage of the opportunity that market bottoms provide, you have to be able to react counterintuitively. In other words, you have to learn to question your "gut," or at least do a better job of interpreting what it's telling you.

Socrates taught us to "know thyself," and this is certainly a valuable piece of advice when it comes to investing. With regard to love and money, however, our strongest impulses can be hard to ignore. It's during those times that you must be able to take a step back and think about what you're doing, think about the meaning of your feelings rather than allowing yourself to simply react.

We are all human, the market can be fickle, and no one is immune. At the beginning of a decline, there is always hope that it will be short-lived, that prices will rebound. Next there is suspicion that we missed out on the highs but can still sell on a rebound. Finally, there is the despair at the realization that there is no way out—typically that is when the panic sales occur, ironically often near the bottom of a market.

One of my favorite *Seinfeld* episodes is the one called "The Opposite." In this episode, George mentions that everything he has ever done, every one of his impulses, has been wrong and has led to failure. With a bolt of insight, he realizes that if he does the opposite, perhaps that will lead to success. And so he proceeds to not only ignore but defy every single instinct he has, down to what he orders for lunch. And amazingly, things do start to turn around for George. All the things he has wanted and never achieved—a beautiful girlfriend, a successful job—all start to miraculously appear.

This episode could have been written about stock market investors because learning how to move counterintuitively is indeed one of the building blocks of success. And just like in another *Seinfeld* episode, "Bizarro Jerry," you will find yourself in the opposite universe and be guided by your opposite self, because the market is bizarro world.

Of course, the pendulum swings equally in both directions. Just because something feels good doesn't mean it's good for you. Lava cake, for example. Or martinis. Early in my career, I had to park on the other side of a small bridge from my office. At the beginning and end of every day I walked over that bridge. It gave me some quality time to think about what I wanted to do each day or what had happened that I had to address tomorrow.

Some days, as I walked across that bridge, I would reflect on a good stock I had bought, and it would give me great pleasure as I added up the hefty profits in my mind. I would imagine how this was just the beginning of many such stellar stocks that I would choose, reaping large returns, and maybe becoming a famous investment advisor based on my uncanny ability to pick a winner.

Amazingly, and probably not coincidently, I would walk into the office after these euphoric crossings to see that my stock had just suddenly dropped through the floor. And I would drop along with it—moving from euphoria to despair in one fell swoop. I learned that just as pain is often a signal that things would soon turn positive, the reverse is often also true, so watch out below!

The question for investors is, how do I understand and interpret my feelings in such a way that I can benefit from them rather than be fooled by them? It took me many years of observation and no small amount of time examining my own emotions to get this right. Part of this study included watching other people. One person in particular that I learned a lot from in this regard was a partner at our firm that we nicknamed "The Trigger."

Inspiring Words You Can Take to the Bank

❝

KNOW WHAT YOU DON'T KNOW

The wise man is one who knows what he does not know.
—ATTRIBUTED TO LAO TZU

Far more money has been lost by investors trying to anticipate corrections, than lost in the corrections themselves.[108]
—PETER LYNCH

When The Trigger says go, I always say no

The Trigger was enamored with trading. He was constantly making little trades, at which he was occasionally successful. Every now and again, though, he got itchy to make a big score—but he was not as good at that. Of course, he conveniently forgot to mention the big trades when he was bragging to us, but why let the facts get in the way of a good sugar high?

"You just have to know how to pull the trigger," he would say, trying to coach us on his brilliant methodology. We all knew that despite his competence at smaller trades, he was terrible at the big ones. It was kind of an inside joke. Every time Trigger would say "pull the trigger," confident that the market was about to move in the direction he predicted, it would invariably do the opposite. The Trigger was a good predictor all right, as long as, like George in the *Seinfeld* episode.[109] you did the opposite of what he told you to do. Sadly, The Trigger never learned from his losses and never realized he was living in bizarro world.

The late nineties were a great time for investors, particularly for technology investors. As shown by the S&P 500, the market went on a run that averaged over a 28% return from 1995 through 1999 with two of those years returning over 30%.[110] This is an almost unbelievable number. The NASDAQ, which is dominated by technology companies, averaged slightly over 40% during the same period, which included an 89% return in 1999.[111]

When you see numbers like this, you know you are walking across that bridge of mine, bathed in a euphoric bubble that is inevitably going to burst at some point, probably when you least expect it. Soaring returns like this are driven by one thing and one thing only—human emotion—and as we all know, feelings change, and the market changes along with them.

The market is emotional

The tech bubble reached such unbelievable heights based on people's excitement and belief that the dream would never end. Folks in those days, in the midst of stunning new technology that nobody really understood, were willing to bank billions on startups that began in somebody's garage because of what they hoped would happen in the future. They were banking on dreams, on potential, not on any actual value. Potential only exists in the human imagination, not on ledger sheets, and yet the market moved on our feelings, not on the numbers.

Tech companies in the last part of the 20th century earned billions for people based on imagination, appreciation, speculation, and illusion. And the market confirmed these illusions day after day. Real companies, such as Apple, Google, Hewlett Packard, and Amazon really had begun as very small companies, some say in a guy's garage, but at the very least by the late nineties were turning into dominant companies.[112] People were asking, "Why not me?" and FOMO set in big time. And many folks that were railing against the trend and pointing to the danger had been wrong for so many years that it was easy to dismiss their cautionary tales.

Even Alan Greenspan, the famed Federal Reserve chairman, who used the term "irrational exuberance"[113] to describe the market back in 1996, was too early to be called accurate. In fact, the market moved strongly upward for years after his dire warning.[114,115] People, even the experts, wanted to believe that the tech dream would go on forever. Nirvana was going to be achieved through the magic of the Internet. Who cares what the balance sheets said?

This incredible time in market history was also a great time for our firm. We avoided the riskiest technology companies, and thus the largest risks and returns, but we were still able to outperform the index each year. Then, as technology began to decline in 2000, we still outperformed by about 12% over the market, putting us in the top decile relative to our peers.

In a way, our company was mirroring the great move in the tech stocks. Our profits were soaring beyond our wildest dreams. Our belief in our investment process was strong and the firm was now being viewed as a new model for investment and corporate strategy. With this stellar record, larger firms came looking to acquire us. However, many of the partners, and especially our infamous Trigger, looked askance at these opportunities for acquisition.

"Why would we sell when things are looking so good?" The Trigger would ask in our meetings. "We can grow ourselves into one of these major firms, we can put Louisville, Kentucky, on the map!" As he said these words, Paul and I exchanged a glance and mouthed the same word to each other: "Trigger!"

When something feels like a sure bet, start to worry

My friend and I felt differently about the acquisition. It wasn't that we had any advance knowledge about when our winning streak might end, or even if it would end. We just intuitively knew by now that when everything feels perfect, that's the time to remind yourself that the only constant in the market is change. Just as we would reassure ourselves in the downtimes that "this too shall pass," the same is inevitably true for the good times. This doesn't mean you have to spend your life nervous about the next shoe dropping, you just have to be agile and ready for change.

Quietly, and without any big arguments, we began to move through the firm's partners, getting them to see that taking the money now would give us freedom from the unknowns. There are always black swans in the offing that would assuredly swoop in at some point. After all, we had history on our side to prove it.

I understood the logic and rationale of those who did not want to sell. There certainly were no problems on the horizon. There were clear skies above, strong winds in our sails, and nothing but friendly seas ahead. If things continued as they were, the potential upside was huge. I could feel the thrill of putting our firm and Louisville on the map of successful investment professionals. Maybe I'd even get on that talk show I had been dreaming of. However, I also remembered Uncle Lew and those predictable noogies. I realized that while I didn't know when this winning streak would end, I did know for sure that it would, and when it did, it would rap its knuckles on my skull if I didn't act like a grownup.

The Trigger never approved of the sale, but we talked enough partners into seeing things from our side that we were able to move forward. Of course, these things don't move without complications and delay. The lawyers had a field day with us, negotiating over the fine details, but eventually we finalized the sale of our firm. It was May of 2001, and just a few months later, on September 11, 2001, the world changed forever, and the market plunged.

Had we waited, had we believed in the illusion of non-stop growth and progress, we would have lost out on the opportunity to capitalize on our success and get while the getting was good. Our firm never would have sold after 9/11 due to the instant crash in the markets, in the economy, and in the going price for investment firms like ours. And unfortunately, as time passed with the acquiring company, our firm began to show some cracks. The team approach we had so carefully constructed, and that had been so instrumental to our market edge, had begun to devolve. We had become too big for our own business model. Ironically, the peak of our firm coincided with the peak of the market. At the time, of course, true to form, The Trigger was asking us, "Why sell now?"

It's tempting to make fun of The Trigger, but the truth is that each of us has an inner Trigger—we are all capable of reacting to market sentiment and allowing our instincts to guide us to do the wrong thing at the wrong time. But if we can admit that we all have it within us to act the fool, then this humility can teach us to hesitate before we act, to consider why we are feeling what we feel.

When we do this, the market can earn us not only profit, but invaluable insight into ourselves.

What I learned from the Tech Boom and Bust

1. **Don't hold big bets in any one market.** Diversify.

2. **When the market moves to such an extreme that you either want to cry uncle or shoot the moon, don't do either thing.** Wait. Then think about it some more before you act.

3. **Point #2 is perhaps one of the most important lessons investors can learn from the large market declines, whether they were the dot-com decline, the financial crisis in 2008, the global pandemic, or whatever may have happened since this writing.** If you felt like crying uncle and selling at some point, it means that you owned too many stocks. Recognize that the time to reduce exposure is not in that time of panic when the market is causing you the most pain. What history has shown us time and time again is that the market will naturally rebound at least to some extent, usually after the last person has capitulated.

4. **Decide what your own risk tolerance is because everyone's is different.** I strongly recommend against letting some advisor or a computer model tell you what risk level will keep you calm when the market turns against you. The best time to determine your risk tolerance is when times are good and most advisors are saying the market has further upside. It is at these calm times that you should imagine the worst. Imagine some terrible surprise and how you would react if all

of a sudden equity prices decline 30% or more. If you believe you would stay strong even then, when not even a significant decline and accompanying bad news would make you cry uncle, then you will have learned the best allocation of stocks for you. Most importantly, it means you will also be holding stocks with strong hands, which means you'll make better decisions in the future when everyone else is ready to surrender.

CHAPTER 10

FIND YOUR SWEET SPOT IN THE MIDDLE

Striking the Balance Between Risk and Safety

My son loved taking bubble baths when he was little. I loved seeing the pure joy on his face as he played with his bath toys, smiling and giggling and full of mischief. He would hide under the bubbles, convinced his mom and I could no longer see him once he had submerged completely beneath the foam. Then he would pop up and surprise us, materializing like a happy creature from the Mr. Bubble lagoon.

One day my son came up from the deep covered in bubbles. "Mom, Dad!" he said, looking at us, delighted with his disguise, "Now I'm white!" Then he sank back under the water, washing the bubbles away and surfaced again. "Back to black," he said. My wife and I looked at each other, and though we both were laughing, it got us thinking too.

I should explain at this juncture that my son is half Chinese, so he had darker skin than the kids in his very white class in Louisville, Kentucky. There had been no reason to talk with him about this, and of course in and of itself was not a big deal, but it did remind us that we were living in a community with very little diversity. We knew that we were the only mixed couple at my company, in our neighborhood, and as far as I could tell, in our whole area of town. It's not that anyone commented on it or treated us differently, but it did make us wonder if diversity was something we should think more about.

It wasn't just the lack of diversity in people, but in cultural experiences and, of course, in food. As my wife so often reminded me, we were hundreds of miles from the nearest decent Chinese restaurant. Kentucky had more than just chop suey in cartons in those days, but Hong was always quick to tell me these dishes were NOT what she meant when she said she was craving Chinese food.

It certainly wasn't just the bubble bath that gave us a wake-up call. Thoughts of our next adventure propelled us into a discussion that had been bubbling just below the surface ever since we moved to Louisville. Remember, as Hong had so directly put it, "I didn't come all the way from China to live in Louisville, Kentucky, for the rest of my life." Of course, we had come to love Louisville, and at the time, the move had made sense because the job made sense. But now that the business had been sold, was this really where we wanted to settle long term?

Inspiring Words You Can Take to the Bank

❝

THE MELTING POT

It is time for parents to teach young people early on that in diversity there is beauty and there is strength.[116]
—MAYA ANGELOU

How can you govern a country which has 246 varieties of cheese?[117]
—CHARLES DE GAULLE

There are not more than five cardinal tastes, yet combinations of them yield more flavors than can ever be tasted.[118]
—SUN TZU, *The Art of War*

"Good morning, Eeyore," said Pooh. "Good morning, Pooh Bear," said Eeyore gloomily. "If it is a good morning, which I doubt," said he. "Why, what's the matter?" "Nothing, Pooh Bear, nothing. We can't all, and some of us don't. That's all there is to it." "Can't all what?" said Pooh, rubbing his nose. "Gaiety. Song-and-dance. Here we go round the mulberry bush."[119]
—A. A. MILNE

Money can't buy you certainty

There were lots of arguments in favor of staying in Louisville. It was a beautiful area, no question, and we had made good friends during our time there. Plus, the cost of living was such that we were potentially set for life after the sale of the company. I still had a good job at a very successful firm, and I felt an obligation to the new owners to continue to help out for the next several years, but after that? In short,

Louisville was safe and secure, but maybe that was the problem. I was beginning to learn that safe and secure isn't the same as feeling happy and fulfilled.

Of course, it's important to note that all of this was happening just after 9/11. It's difficult to evoke the horrific shock that tragedy registered in real time. It was a jarring experience that changed the world for a lot of us, probably all of us in some way whether we realized it or not. It was one of those moments that draws a bright line through the course of human experience. There was life before 9/11, and then there is life now. Like most Americans at the time, I was feeling all kinds of anxiety from so many sources.

Some of it, I think, had to do with the erosion of American exceptionalism that I had been brought up believing in. War was not supposed to be able to reach our shining shores, of this we had all been certain. And yet somehow, it had. American invulnerability had toppled, and so it was hard to trust the ground beneath my feet. I struggled to take anything for granted—even the principles of aerodynamics. It was a strange way to feel on the heels of the biggest financial windfall of my life. Instead of certainty, what I felt was free-floating anxiety and even fear. For example, I had flown all my life, and yet suddenly, I was fearful on airplanes. I would look around at my fellow passengers and wonder which one might send the plane crashing down.

During this time, I experimented with new methods of handling my underlying anxiety. I learned to meditate, thinking that it would help me recover my inner balance. I had always thought of meditation as a road to enlightenment, a transformation into a higher level of existence. I imagined grand masters, wise and calm, meditating on the top of some impassable peak, at one with the universe. What I discovered was that, for me anyway, meditation was mostly just sitting. I would sit for 15 to 20 minutes each day, allow thoughts to come in and go out without judgment, and though this sounds somewhat simple, this began a journey of a more peaceful time for me.

Somehow, that time I set aside to let my thoughts drift without judgment, did make me feel calmer, more balanced, and more creative in my daily life. Without any particular moment of great awakening, I noticed myself changing.

My daily meditation practice allowed me to accept uncertainty, to live without having to be sure, and, as a result, to be more present and appreciative in the moment. I began to focus on enjoying what I did have, instead of fearing what I might lose if the worst happened. And that made me a better person—and a better investor.

Gradually, I began to fear less and enjoy more. And I realized that I had plenty to enjoy. I had two young and healthy boys, a happy marriage, a job I loved, and a safety net in my bank account. In other words, I had it knocked. I had managed to wrap my arms around the American Dream. I had made it home free. And yet, something was missing, and it was bigger than just a quest for better Chinese food— although that was definitely a factor.

Unconsciously up until this point, my wife and I had been seeking out some spice in our lives, and we weren't finding it in Louisville. We had gone too conservative, our lives had become too predictable, we were too safe. Ironically, now we didn't feel safe at all, so what was the point of a safe harbor? We decided to court some risk. We weren't thinking of jumping out of airplanes or helicopter skiing or anything like that, but we did wonder if there was a place for us to live that would better fit our dreams. First, we had to figure out exactly what our dreams were. And that of course, took some time.

A good investor always knows when to leave

The bubble-bath epiphany was one of several things that let us know that now was the time for planning to make a move and strike a better balance between risk and safety in our lives. Over the next couple of years, we took some trips and tried to sample as much of what our big country had to offer us as we possibly could. We traveled to the West Coast on vacation and wherever we went, we would spend a day with a real estate agent looking for places that we might like to live. We spent time in Portland, Seattle, San Francisco, and Newport Beach, and though each seemed fun and exciting, we never got that feeling that this was the sweet spot that we wanted to call home.

Then, we visited San Diego and although we and the kids had a great time, none of the houses the agent showed us felt like THE house. It was the last day of the trip, and we were visiting one of my wife's friends that she had known in China. As they showed us around their neighborhood, we came upon an open house. The moment I walked through the door I just knew we had found our place. Fortunately, my wife felt the same way.

We talked about it at the airport and decided that we should just email a low-ball bid and see what happened. And as you might guess, upon landing in Louisville, we had a call from the agent to say we had just bought a house in San Diego. I wasn't known for making spontaneous decisions, and maybe compared to other people this wasn't lightning fast, but for me it was a huge and sudden move.

While the deal happened quickly, it took some time for us to physically make the move. The kids were in school, and we wanted them to finish out the year. The house needed work and I had to unwind what I was doing at the firm, although they did ask me to stay on at a distance for at least year. Everything seemed to just naturally fall into place. It was as if we were finally on the path we were meant to follow.

Looking back, I credit my agility to the balance I had found in my life and the safety net I had built, which allowed over-cautious me to stretch forward, to reach up and out of my box, and take a leap of faith. Without these things, I might have been more reticent and missed out on a chance to find the kind of certainty that only comes from knowing you're doing exactly the right thing for you, so when opportunity unexpectedly knocks, you are willing and able to open the door.

Finding balance is a big part of my philosophy as an investor and investment advisor. Part of finding this balance goes back to an age-old argument between my grandpa and my Uncle Ralph. This mostly good-natured debate rumbled on for most of my young life. Uncle Ralph and Grandpa were alike in many ways. They were exactly the same height, were both loving and caring family men, and both their wives adored them. Neither wife put up with their foolishness, and so they behaved themselves for the most part. They put a lot of stock in their view of the world, and while they agreed on a lot, when it came to money and investment, they were like chalk and cheese.

Try to travel in the center lane if you want to go the distance

Grandpa was a middle-of-the-road man. He never shot the moon. He believed in taking a few profits off the top when his stocks would rally, but his approach was always moderate, always controlled. When Uncle Ralph would tease him about tossing nickels around like they were manhole covers, the dialogue would go something like this.

"Ralph, the market is like a golf ball, what goes up is going to come down. In the meantime, I take a little off the table, trim my profits, but 1 don't sell the whole position, and I let the stock keep growing. So if it drops, I'm safe, and at least I've enjoyed a little of my success before the ball comes down in the sand trap."

"Either you like a stock or you don't!" Uncle Ralph would counter. "It's either a buy or a sell—there's no in between. Rather than a 'stop loss' philosophy, yours sounds more like a 'stop gain' philosophy!" I will never sell a stock that I like. I go big or I go home."

"That is, if you've still got a home."

Grandpa would always smile in a way that said he was kidding but not kidding. I would sit and listen to these two go back and forth from the time I was too young to really understand what they were disagreeing about. Still, I knew something was happening between two of my favorite people—I was what my grandpa called a little pitcher with big ears. And through the years, as I matured and began to understand their discussions, they became a sort of school of opposing influences that helped me to shape where I would ultimately fall on the risk spectrum.

★ ★ ★ **Movies on the Money** ★ ★ ★

Legend of Bagger Vance (2000)[120]

DIRECTOR: *Robert Redford*

STARS: *Will Smith, Matt Damon, Charlize Theron*

A down and out golfer attempts to redeem his game and his life with the help of a metaphysical caddy. The movie relates the mental aspect of the golf game to our lives and reminds us that often the answer to the question of which path to choose—just like our golf swing is our own—has always been within us and is for us alone to discover.

Extremely Loud and Incredibly Close (2011)[121]

DIRECTOR: *Stephen Daldry*

STARS: *Thomas Horn, Tom Hanks, Sandra Bullock*

Once again, a Tom Hanks movie reminds us about the resilience of the human spirit in this story about a nine-year-old boy and amateur sleuth, who finds a mysterious key left behind by his father who died in 9/11. This movie does a great job of making us confront and consider all the questions left unanswered by the people we lost in the towers.

Worth (2020)[122]

DIRECTOR: *Sara Colangelo*

STARS: *Michael Keaton, Amy Ryan, Stanley Tucci*

Based on a true story, *Worth* follows the efforts of Ken Feinberg, an attorney who must calculate the value of every human life lost in 9/11 in order to distribute the $9 billion victims' compensation fund. A great look at the enormous and incalculable value of a single human life senselessly lost in the attack on the towers.

There's little room for error when you're traveling in the fast lane

My Uncle Ralph was a legendary iconoclast. His epic quips were a classic commentary on life, combining humor and insight. He watched a jogger once and said, "Those runners with those pained faces, they might think they're going to live longer, but I think their suffering will just make their lives *seem* longer." Once at a Yom Kippur service, he turned to me during the congregation's communal confession, which had them confessing to all kinds of things—lying, breach of trust, lustful desires, excessive drinking and eating, evil thoughts, deceit, scheming, embezzlement, and on and on. You name it, they confessed to it. It was the day of atonement after all. Finally, at the very end of a very long list, my uncle turned to me and said in a voice loud enough to draw a look that could kill from my aunt, "Mick, let's get of here, these folks are terrible people. Definitely not our crowd!"

He wasn't afraid of the rabbis, or the police, or the stock market. Even robbers didn't scare off Uncle Ralph's sense of irony. I lived with my aunt and uncle in Cincinnati right after college, and one evening, my aunt and I came home to discover that their house had been ransacked. We called the police but once we looked around, we realized that nothing had been stolen. When my uncle came home, the police told him what happened, and that fortunately for him, nothing appeared to be missing.

"Honey, this is insulting," he said, looking genuinely offended. "What, we have nothing worth stealing? Now I really am mad!" It took a minute for the police to understand my uncle was just joking. Then a look of panic came over his face. He rushed into the bedroom and came out clutching an envelope and looking enormously relieved.

"Thank God," he said, "the Bengals tickets are still here…" That one got a smile out of the police, who were undoubtedly Bengals fans as well, but earned him yet another withering look from my aunt.

My uncle had one main priority, his family, and everything else was fair game. He'd make a joke about anything, and his money management was just as edgy as his humor. I was fascinated by his attitude on things, and by his uncanny ability to gamble it all and win big. In fact, as I got older, my aunt told me that Uncle Ralph was in fact, a real gambler when he was younger, and often quite successful. As time went on, his bets got larger and larger. His winnings paid for trips and all kinds of luxuries, but the losses stung too. Finally, my aunt just couldn't take the big swings any longer, and she gave him an ultimatum: "Either the gambling goes, or I do!"

My fun Uncle Ralph and my Aunt Carol who loved each other deeply

Their love for each other was deep and in this case, love won out. Outside of his Saturday bridge game, my uncle's gambling stopped, until, of course, he had had saved enough money to start investing in stocks, which somehow flew beneath my aunt's radar. As I became more experienced in the market, my uncle and I enjoyed sharing investment ideas. He was actually a great student of the game, doing his own research and in our discussions often knew more about a company's earnings projections and products than I did. Of course, he was also looking for stocks that not only had large upside because of potential risk, but he often had concentrated positions and when they worked out could result in big returns. It was not a low-risk strategy, but though we had different ways to go about investing, it did teach me to be open to other's ideas as his successes taught me much about risk taking.

The middle lane gives you more options when traffic hits a snag

My grandpa, on the other hand, was a man who believed in equilibrium. He took over a furniture factory at an early age and was very successful, managing to keep his workers happy during a time of great upheaval between union and management. He had a canny knack of knowing how to balance the interests of opposing camps. Grandpa always said the key to good relationships was listening to everybody and finding just the right spot between them.

During the war, he transitioned his company from manufacturing furniture to manufacturing bulletproof vests. Not only was this an agile pivot that allowed his business to survive hard times, but it also gave him an opportunity to serve his country in a time of war. My grandpa himself was a bulletproof vest. Of course, he was not all warm hugs and understanding. Where my uncle was edgy with his humor, my grandpa was edgy with the unvarnished truth.

When my mom was going through the divorce, she asked him to go talk to my dad to see if there was a chance for reconciliation and ask him to come home. "Honey, he's a good man but he's moved on," my grandpa told my mom evenly. "The sooner you accept that, the better. You don't want a man who doesn't love you. You will find love again, but not with him." That may have been the only time I saw my mom get visibly angry at her father. In the end, though, even she had to admit he was right—she did move on, and she did find love again.

It was my grandpa who taught me how to play golf. As a kid I always thought it was boring but as I got older, I began to see the subtleties of the game and the many life lessons one could learn from the sport. I wound up loving golf and teaching it to my own sons. My grandpa's golf style mirrored his lifestyle. He was a middle-of-the-fairway guy. He didn't take unnecessary risks, stayed clear of the traps, and didn't try to skirt the margins. He also knew how to take joy in the game— to let himself relax, set his mind free from worries, and really enjoy it. That being said, he did have some great successes, such as hitting a hole in one at the age of 85! At that time, his eyesight was so bad, neither he nor his friends saw the ball go in and he apparently looked for that ball for 10 minutes before his friend said, "Marc, check the damned hole!"

My ever-patient grandpa

When he was teaching me to swing, he told me that a golf swing, like life, was a pendulum. The idea was to be able to use just the right amount of pressure to get the job done. The skill was in moving between extremes without losing your balance. Of course, I was young, swinging hard every time, rarely connecting, trying my hardest to impress him, and not doing much of anything well at all. As he watched me, he'd try to coach me and eventually throw up his hands and say, "Quit listening to my advice and just hit the damned ball!" We'd both laugh and then I'd relax and more times than not I'd hit my best shot of the day.

Although my grandfather was a man with a great deal of patience, I managed to test it. Whenever I'd take my time with a swing, he would get exasperated with me and give me advice I wish all golfers would heed. "Kid," he'd say, and put his hand on my back to urge me forward so we could get it over with already. "It's not bad to be bad, just don't be slow!"

I enjoyed learning from both my grandpa and my uncle and from seeing both sides of the argument. It was clear that both had been amazingly successful with their opposing approaches, but ultimately it was my grandpa's sense of balance, embedded in my DNA, that took hold of me as I became an investment professional. On the other hand, I had a little bit of my Uncle Ralph's panache to remind me not to be too safe or too afraid of risk, because I might miss out on a lot of fun and laughs and some unique opportunities.

In the end, Uncle Ralph had to admit that Grandpa had been at least a little right, but it took the collapse of a market sector to get him to admit that he might have been wrong. As tech stocks ran in the late nineties, I would tell Uncle Ralph how we were starting to cut back and take some profits, even as we were keeping our long-term positions. I heard myself sounding just like my grandpa, trying unsuccessfully to win the same debate that he had always tried, and failed, to win. My uncle's philosophy remained unchanged. He said he loved his tech stocks and was going to hold on, despite the fact that tech stocks dominated his portfolio. And even when tech started declining, he continued to hold on.

Unfortunately, tech stocks continued to tumble, and my uncle had no safety net. Even more frightening, he had retired and was dependent on his stock profits to live on. He had once told me he didn't believe in bonds or worrying about generating income from his investments. "Bonds are too slow," he told me. "Why bother with them when you can live on the profits from stocks?" These turned out to be fateful words.

He finally reached his breaking point as the tech bubble crumbled. He told me that he still had enough money to live on, but if stocks dropped further, it would threaten his lifestyle and maybe his future. And who knows what my aunt might have said or done then. So, with a little humility, my uncle sold, although it was near the bottom. He had protected his retirement with my aunt and still had enough in stocks to make a comeback. Some piece of the gambler in him would just never say die.

My uncle finally understood how ignoring the idea of downside discipline meant destabilizing his safety net. In the end, he did make a great comeback. He changed his style to one that would allow him to take great risks with much of his money but retain enough of a safety net to prevent a catastrophe. He had found his sweet spot in the middle.

I saw a great change in my uncle after this. Even though he still allowed his betting instincts to dominate his decisions, he was more measured and had adopted some of my grandpa's agility. When stocks started falling during the banking crisis in 2008, he quickly sold his bank stocks and was able to keep most of his profits. He started buying early as stocks bottomed, and I was shocked to learn how much Apple he owned as the market rallied.

Of course, he would say, "I like Apple so why shouldn't it dominate my portfolio? And why would I ever sell when I still like the stock?" That part hadn't changed, but he also had another portion of his account that was safe. He had diversified with stocks like Procter & Gamble and Johnson & Johnson, boring stocks in his opinion but even he would admit, necessary. He had learned, as I learned after 9/11, that while a financial safety cushion will never make you feel perfectly and globally safe, it will give you the increased agility you need to fill in the gaps and the willingness to stretch forward in order to find your proper balance. In my case, it was buying a house on the fly in San Diego, California, the land of swimming pools and movie stars that I had always equated with my definition of success, which turned out to be my sweet spot in the middle.

Observing and sharing with my uncle and my grandfather taught me that with diversification and downside discipline you can blend any number of investment strategies and still be successful. Although Uncle Ralph was by nature more aggressive and a greater risk-taker than I was, it was only by finding the right balance, his own sweet spot in the middle, that he was able to achieve his goals and maintain the safety net he needed to survive the downdrafts.

I realize that my sweet spot in the middle is unique to me. Everybody has their own version. We all have our unique threshold for risk, pain points we can't cross, and it's critical for each of us to know where and what they are. By really knowing ourselves and finding that balance, we can enjoy what we have while still being able to take chances to optimize our growth.

At the age of 87, my grandpa had a stroke. It happened, naturally, on the golf course, where his last conscious thought likely occurred, and which I'm sure is how he would have wanted it. He lingered on for just a few days afterward, so I was able to visit him in the hospital. Each member of the family took turns to make sure he was never alone. During my visits, I would read him poetry as I knew that was what he always enjoyed, though he showed no sign of consciousness.

In my final hour with him, I had a premonition that it might be the last time I saw him. I ended the poetry reading and then I expressed all the love I felt for him, letting him know how important he had been to me. I told him that his house was always filled with warmth, that I treasured the special times I'd spent with him and the lessons he'd taught me. I don't know if he heard me, and I'm not sure it mattered. I felt better that I told him how grateful I was for our relationship. Then I kissed his forehead and began to walk away. As an afterthought, I turned around in the doorway and said, "And I'll always remember that my golf swing, like my life, is a pendulum..." I swear, after I said that, my grandpa smiled.

Inspiring Words You Can Take to the Bank

"

Investing should be more like watching paint dry or watching grass grow. If you want excitement, take $800 and go to Las Vegas.[123]
—PAUL SAMUELSON

If you can't sleep at night because of your stock market position, then you have gone too far. If this is the case, then sell your position down to the sleeping level.[124]
—EDWIN LEFÈVRE, *Reminiscences of a Stock Operator*, 1923

The stock market is a device to transfer money from the impatient to the patient.[125]
—WARREN BUFFETT

What I learned From My Even-Keel Grandpa and My Crazy-Like-a-Fox Uncle Ralph

During our heyday in the nineties, our strategy of multiple attribute diversification helped us not only to be able to conservatively outperform the market, but it also struck a nice note for new and old clients alike. They felt comfortable because they saw consistent returns and their downside was minimized because of the built-in diversification.

This strategy has also allowed me to blend what I had learned through the years all the way back to the benign neglect strategy I practiced with Eloise, my very first client. We could hold long-term stocks that were conservative with consistent earnings and still get in on new growth stocks. This strategy allowed a margin for error. We could take risks with a safety net. This blending seemed to fit all different types of markets. It's what my grandpa understood. He knew how to take a long view, to be conservative but still nimble enough to respond to unexpected eventualities on the green.

Here is the Multiple Attribute Diversification blend:

1. Buy some growth stocks that are risky and have more upside.

2. Buy some low PE stocks that are less volatile and energetic but can rally if the economy is doing well.

3. Buy some higher-yield stocks that help provide income but are protected on the downside.

4. Hold on to some cash and bonds to help protect you and to help you meet your long-term objectives.

CHAPTER 11

ALWAYS CHOOSE FACT OVER FICTION

The Get Real Guide to Mellowing Your Money

Over almost two and a half centuries the American Dream has taken on different guises and personalities, complete with tokens of affluence and success that make us feel wealthy and ensure that the neighbors know that we've arrived. Maybe we have a home in Beverly Hills, so we are living the dream. We own a Model T Ford, so we are living the dream. In times past maybe we had a refrigerator, a television, or a piano in the parlor. All of these, at one time, were status symbols.

One status symbol that has never gone out of style is the great American steakhouse. The Pine Club,[126] the best steakhouse in Dayton, Ohio, at one point rated the second best in America and which has been serving up well-marbled porterhouses seared since 1947, is one such timeless palace of American plenty.

When I was young, if there was an important birthday, promotion, graduation, or engagement to celebrate, we would go to the Pine Club. It was the place you went to make things feel special, and they knew it. They didn't take reservations, they did not take bribes at the door, and they only accepted cash. On such occasions, I can still remember my dad telling my mom in the morning, "Now don't be late picking me up! You know what can happen after five o'clock at the Pine Club!" What he meant was that if you got there much past five o'clock, you potentially had a two-hour wait in front of you or maybe longer. It would be worth the wait, but that sounded like an eternity to a growing boy.

My dad was punctual, so we were never late, but I can remember the look of pure disappointment on the faces of diners who pulled up at a quarter past five. Nobody left, no matter how long the line was. By five-thirty, you could barely see to the other side of the bar, so thick was the air with a nutty haze from the patient people smoking and drinking scotch on the rocks while waiting for their tables.

The Pine Club has never changed—still no reservations, still only takes cash. In fact, when George Bush came to eat there many years ago, they said great, but you better wait! Naturally, the Secret Service held Bush's place in line at the bar.[127] The Pine Club has remained relevant and desired across almost seven decades and it's a great comfort to me every time I go back there to know that some things stay the same, some American institutions remain unbowed.

The piano in the parlor was another supreme status symbol of its day, and the only form of family entertainment before the phonograph made its grand entrance onto the domestic stage. What was once the province of royalty and nobles became the instrument of democracy in America, reinforced and repurposed through American ingenuity.

So sturdy were these new American pianos that they could be found in parlors from the White House to log cabins on the prairie to gold prospector's shacks in the highest peaks of the Rocky Mountains.

The Baldwin Piano Company, located where I used to work in Cincinnati, Ohio, was the first company to make pianos accessible to the middle class. They did this by allowing families to finance the purchase, so pianos quite literally became a financial instrument. They adopted the financing strategy that Singer sewing machines, at an earlier time, had tried unsuccessfully to institute, using what was essentially a consignment/installment plan and through this financing, grow their piano business and their financing business simultaneously. In fact, many families felt that an investment in a piano was a safe way to harbor assets during uncertain times, as if a piano were a precious metal like gold or silver.

By the early 20th century, Baldwin had become the largest piano retailer in a country that held the corner on the market.[128,129,130,131] The vision of families gathering around the piano while Mom played and Dad and the kids sang along was, like the Pine Club, a nostalgic vision of a happier and more innocent America. Of course, we know it masked other problems and challenges our country was undergoing, but the image gave comfort to many. Life seemed simple, steaks were rare, and bars were a biohazard. Nobody could resist an image like that, no matter where you lived in the world.

Don't let them pull legacy

I first became acquainted with The Baldwin Piano Company at a lunch meeting being held by an investment analyst from out of town. As a junior analyst, working long hours for short pay, there are few things more exciting than knowing that an analyst was rolling into town and throwing a luncheon. Even if it meant going out with your boss, it meant a chance to hear new ideas, and more importantly, eat and drink on somebody else's tab. On this occasion, my boss was unable to join us due to another engagement. So the two young analysts were going to an all-you-can-eat shindig, unchaperoned. Nothing could be finer.

Before we left, Ken told us that the talk would focus on a local company that had just pivoted and was causing quite a stir as a result. Baldwin United, he explained, was originally a traditional piano manufacturer, but in more recent years had been transitioning into a more complicated business model. Under the guidance of its visionary CEO, Baldwin became a standout stock performer.

Baldwin United traced its roots all the way back to D.H. Baldwin, which had been operating in Cincinnati since the early 1900s. Although the company had built its reputation on piano manufacturing and retailing, during World War II it transitioned its factories into making airplane parts. After the war, they pivoted again and went right back to making quality pianos, which attracted the attention of such famous musicians over the years as Leonard Bernstein, Dave Brubeck, Lawrence Welk, Carly Simon, Bruce Hornsby, and even Liberace.

So, although its most recent incarnation had created a lot of controversy in the financial press, reimagining itself was in Baldwin United's DNA, and becoming a financial company wasn't really that much of a stretch.

Through their acquisitions, Baldwin became a major player in the financial services industry, controlling over 200 insurance companies[132] and even taking over Sperry & Hutchinson,[133] best known for another nostalgic American kitchen table icon, S&H Green Stamps. Baldwin followed up this acquisition by acquiring (MGIC) the Mortgage Guarantee Insurance Company,[134] which was top in the mortgage financing field at that time.

Morley Thompson,[135] Baldwin United's chairman and CEO, was known as somewhat of a financial magician and he proved it with this purchase. He had to work with eight separate banks to fund the $1.2 billion price tag.[136] Unfortunately, it was at a time with volatile interest rates and with a drop in MGIC's profits,[137] there was a hint that clouds might be gathering on the horizon for the mighty and agile Baldwin Piano Company.

In fact, one young analyst who worked for *Barron's* at the time, Jim Chanos,[138] had begun to sniff out the problems in Baldwin's accounting as early as 1982, declaring the firm a "house of cards." He contended that Baldwin was "doomed to collapse due to over-leveraged, kinky accounting, and negative cash flow." His criticism was met mostly with derision, particularly by other Wall Street analysts who had been recommending the stock.

Believe half of what you read and little of what you hear at an industry luncheon with an open bar

Such was the landscape when my fellow junior associate and I attended that food, booze, and invest-athon lunch. Baldwin was already in the midst of a controversy, and the stock had begun to drop due to some of Chanos' articles[139] and the rumors that they had inspired.

The investment analyst who was speaking told us that *Barron's* had it all wrong. Baldwin was a strong company, she said, with roots that stretched deep into the substrate of America—it was practically knit into the business DNA of the nation.[140] She argued that Baldwin had been in the financial services business all along and there was nothing to worry about. My colleague and I listened closely, well, as closely as one could listen, given the three martinis we had ordered at lunch. And of course, the analyst turned out to be a beautiful woman, who had also brought along the famous magician himself, Morley Thompson, as a surprise guest.

Morley Thompson was a legend in Cincinnati at the time and so when he got up and echoed the analyst's thoughts and conclusions, my colleague and I were sold on the strength of Baldwin stock, hook, line, and sinker. Of course, we were also tipsy and stuffed to the gills on banquet chicken and had spent the last hour staring at the beautiful woman at the table. By the time lunch was over, we were true believers, ready to go back and evangelize the Baldwin gospel.

When you feel an urgency, slow down

I remember walking out of that meeting with a firm resolve. We were clear what our next steps were. We floated back to the office on a cloud of gin and nostalgia, ready to convince our senior research partner of the greatness of Baldwin United stock and get him to let us start buying it for our clients that very afternoon, by the bucketful. I remember we were in a real hurry to purchase before anyone else could begin to accumulate the stock at these bargain prices.

We entered the partner's office, hopes and enthusiasm high, and began to relay what we had just learned and how much we wanted to buy in to the dream. The partner had great patience and listened intently. He too had a practiced pause, learned from our big boss, Ken, that could really drive you crazy when you were in a hurry. When we finished, he looked us in the eye, wait for it, wait for it, wait for it…

"Sounds very interesting, boys," he said finally. "But I'm curious. How does Baldwin United make money?" This question, while simple on the surface, sobered us up pretty quickly, because we realized we couldn't answer him. We knew that the big story at Baldwin was no longer pianos, but what was it again? We couldn't remember. The partner watched us struggling, smiled, and kindly let us off the hook.

"I've learned one thing the hard way, guys," he said. "Never buy anything when you don't clearly understand how they make their money. I don't have to grasp every technical detail and nuance, but I should know how the company turns a buck."

This stopped us both in our tracks as we realized that we clearly had no understanding at all of how Baldwin United was going to turn a profit. And, as it turned out, neither did the analysts who were recommending the stock. And neither did their chairman, the great magician, Morley Thompson.

You have to know how a company makes money

Fortunately for us, we were not allowed to buy Baldwin stock, which saved our investors their money and us some genuine embarrassment and maybe even our jobs. Shortly after that infamous liquid luncheon, Baldwin United stock went into free fall.[141] It turned out that the young analyst from *Barron's* that everyone had ignored, and that Baldwin had even sued, had been right all along. Baldwin was a house of cards, and no magician, not even Morley Thompson, can defy gravity forever without an exit plan. Baldwin became the largest bankruptcy in America at that time.[142]

Unfortunately, many of our fellow junior and senior associates who attended the luncheon that day did not have our research partner's foresight or discipline. Thousands of shares were bought as a result of the chairman's performance, and assurance that everything was fine when quite obviously behind the scenes they were not going well at all. I believe three things were working against those that ended up believing in Baldwin that day, dangerous influences that made us all feel comfortable and even excited about buying a dud.

1. **A Sentimental Journey**

   First, they had the legacy of the original Baldwin product in their minds, the world's most resilient, adaptable, and aspirational pianos, where the upwardly mobile American families of a golden age gone by gathered to sing a common song. And Baldwin also held S&H Green Stamps, another sentimental trigger for memories of a gentler and more innocent time that probably never really existed.

   Who at the luncheon that day didn't have a memory of sitting with their mother or grandmother at the kitchen table as a child, licking and pasting those green stamps into books that could be turned into all manner of miraculous new thingamajigs for the home? This kind of warm, fuzzy nostalgia made us all want to be a part of that dream again, to invest in its future.

But when you really think about it, in the sober light of day after a boozy luncheon, is it ever a good idea to invest in the past?

2. **Wall Street Legitimacy**

The other trend that slanted the playing field in Baldwin's favor that day was that they had the might of Wall Street on their side. Even though the company had changed, H&S Green Stamps and MGIC mortgage products felt safe, had performed well historically, and seemed reliable. Wall Street vouched for them, which to us meant that seasoned analysts had dug into the fine details of their corporate reports. How could they have missed any treachery? But of course, they did, they missed it entirely.

3. **Celebrity Influencer**

Finally, we had the charisma of the chairman of the board, the late, great Morley Thompson himself. This heady cocktail (literally and figuratively) produced an alchemy capable of pulling a veil over even the most experienced analyst's judgment. That veil made us forget to ask the simple question: How do you plan to make money?

This was a powerful lesson for me, and one I called upon years later, when the wisdom you gain from watching the disintegration of an American legacy brand from close up came in handy. As did the experience of coming within a whisper of being part of its downfall. I am of course, referring to that great big beautiful and inscrutable black box in the sky: Enron.

Why Enron's magical black box fooled many

Just to set the scene once again, the go-go years of the late nineties was a time when technology stocks were flying high on creative financing, and few were asking how anybody was going to turn a profit. It seemed immaterial, considering the movement in some of the stocks. People were buying and selling big dreams. The bottom line was floating in the sky, defying gravity, and few thought it would ever fall back to earth. Creativity and aspiration for the future of technology reigned supreme. Nothing could stop us now.

Ironically, in this startup climate, Enron was a combination of two dinosaurs, two natural gas companies—Houston Natural Gas,[143] (HNG) formed in 1940, and InterNorth, which started as Northern Natural Gas, formed in 1930. Both were very traditional companies that benefited from the commodity surge in the 1970s. The merger was designed to help two pipeline companies with good synergy to combine and create the second largest pipeline in the US at the time.

In 1985 Ken Lay[144] took over and in the 1990s changed the nature of this traditional company by turning energy into a tradeable commodity. Profits began to climb and so did the stock price. Enron even began to enter the fiber optics cable market and combined profits in this market with their profits from trading energy. With this novel approach, Enron became a darling of Wall Street and even won the most innovative company award for six consecutive years. Naturally, the stock price climbed, eventually almost quintupling in price and becoming one of the top stocks in the S&P 500 by the late 1990s.

Our stock team missed the runup in Enron from the beginning. We didn't envision that the company was more than a slow-growing natural gas pipeline company and found other stocks we liked better. As the stock rose and became one of the top winners, people—and by people, I mean some of our noisier clients along with some partners—began to ask us why we were ignoring such an innovative and successful company. Why were we missing the boat? The Trigger was practically chomping at the bit, begging us to buy.

Despite The Trigger's voracious interest, we did take the concerns seriously. A team of us studied Enron and were tempted by the glowing reports and the bright future that Enron envisioned as they continued to expand into other businesses and new verticals. During one discussion, a team member looked up and asked, "I know what the analysts are saying but do we really know how Enron is making money? I mean, can we really see it?"

And in that one moment, my mind went straight back to our flirtation with disaster and Baldwin United over 10 years earlier. We decided against buying Enron stock. Just as we had resisted the siren's call of the past with Baldwin, we resisted the siren's call of the future with Enron, and thereby averted catastrophe. Our magical incantation that dispersed the veil came down to one simple question: How does the company make money?

The most dangerous words in investment are "This time it's different"

Most of us remember what happened to Enron.[145,146] Within a year, the stock began falling apart, and the news leaked that—like Baldwin years before—Enron was a house of cards built on "creative accounting" (read "cooked books") and the inability of outside analysts to see through the chimera of hope and nostalgia that the company's officers had manufactured.

Sure, throughout history, products have always failed, and companies have gone bust. This has been happening for centuries. But it does seem that over this most recent cycle, a lot of legacy businesses have been shipwrecked on the shores of hubris thanks to their leadership. Once solid companies are reaching outside of their area of expertise and using the loyalty and fidelity of their shareholders, who don't question their expertise, to sail the ship into unfamiliar seas because their CEO has dreams and ambition, only to sink beneath the waves when the truth comes to light.

Just say no to FOMO

From my vantage point, since the early eighties we have entered a period of willingness to buy what we do not know and don't understand. As investors, we have become more willing to take risks due to FOMO than to go the conservative route and possibly forgo future gains. Discipline, restraint, and balance all sound very boring in this boom-and-bust market. There's no thrill in the middle of the road. Or is there? I guess it depends on what you mean by "missing out," and what you mean by "thrilling." It's the argument that Grandpa and Uncle Ralph are still probably having in the afterlife.

And this, of course, leads us inexorably to the Bernie Madoff scandal.[147] Here again, individuals and large institutions were willing to invest money based on the charisma of one man, in a product they knew nothing about, solely through fear of missing out. Bernie was selling the impossible. He was guaranteeing a return that was not even reasonable given the volatility of the market. Yet for so many years he had been delivering this return theoretically, and people began to believe what in their heads they must have known was impossible.

It was, of course, merely a creative reimagining of reality that existed only on paper, but this was enough for people to suspend their disbelief and line up to buy into the dream. People get this crazy idea in their heads over and over again that there might be something magical, something only one person can do, something beyond profit, that will drive profit. What all these examples show is that the only thing that drives profit is profit.

As I write this, GameStop stock is selling another dream, the democratization of the market. Cryptocurrency[148] is also making a move and history is not fully written on this score, but I have a feeling I've seen this movie before. Fear and novelty, hope and nostalgia can drive assets higher for a time.

Baldwin and Enron made spectacular gains before they folded. And some investors made it out before the stocks completely collapsed. Some even made great profits and lived to tell how they rode the bronco, got out before the bell rang, and lived to tell the tale. More did not.

Inspiring Words You Can Take to the Bank

"

THE SONG REMAINS THE SAME

There is nothing new in Wall Street. There can't be because speculation is as old as the hills. Whatever happens in the stock market today has happened before and will happen again.[149]

—EDWIN LEFÈVRE, *Reminiscences of a Stock Operator*, 1923

I put two children through Harvard by trading options. Unfortunately, they were my broker's children.[150]

—JASON ZWEIG

Your visions will become clear only when you can look into your own heart. Who looks outside, dreams; who looks inside, awakes.[151]

—C.G. JUNG

Rules for Buying and Not Buying the American Dream

1. **Know what you own:** Knowing what we own doesn't guarantee success with every purchase, but it can help us avoid the catastrophes and losses that may take years to recover from. This knowledge also gives us the security and confidence we need when the tide turns.

2. **Don't listen to the screaming headlines or the excited experts:** All stocks have ups and downs, and they rarely occur without some headline or some analyst explaining what is going wrong and causing fear in the minds of the investor. If

we know why we own a stock or a fund, we can better hold on through these down moves, ignore the noise and the fears that are circulating, and ride out the storm.

3. **Know what is coming and what is going out:** If we own funds, we should look at expenses and what type of stocks are being held. It is easy to look at performance and chase what has been acting well, but this is, in essence, just chasing a dream because past performance is not an indicator. Just because a fund has done well doesn't mean it will do well going forward. The only way to know this is to look at what a fund holds and whether the stocks fit long-term goals or whether they are more speculative, or somewhere in between. I found that when I know what I own, when I know why a stock is going to eventually grow, then I have strong hands and can hold for the long term despite near-term volatility.

4. **Think before you leap:** Many of us are prone to speculate at times, and some speculations will be successful. It's okay to take a leap every so often but do it consciously. When we understand that we have entered the realm of speculation, we have to abide by different rules. We should be willing to take some profits along the way more quickly. We should be willing to bail out at signs of trouble. We should be more willing to give up hope and not be taken in by the charisma of a particular corporate leader or analyst who reassures us that all is well. Don't take them at their word—do your research and listen to what your brain is telling you.

5. **Always take the long view:** Remember who you are and what you are trying to accomplish. By taking the long view, we can watch with curiosity how others rise and fall with the winds of

speculation, but we won't have to experience the pain of great loss that we will not recover from.

Helpful Hints for Investors Who Want to Use Advisors, Mutual Funds, or Exchange Traded Funds

It's okay to delegate the "knowing what you own" part of the equation to advisors or by owning diversified mutual funds or ETFs (Exchange Traded Funds). Many investors are quite successful this way and either don't have the time or interest to know every stock. If this is the case, below are some of the questions that will help you have confidence that your portfolio will meet your own unique objectives and risk tolerance level:

1. **What is your long-term objective and how much risk can you stand in order to achieve it?**

   Many of the stories in this book focus on what happens when we don't consider our objectives or our risk tolerance. Whether we are managing our own money or working with an advisor, it is critical that we establish these guidelines first and don't be swayed by good or bad headlines, neighbors bragging about their cryptocurrency profits, or embarrassment about our risk-averse nature. Decide, based on worst-case outcomes, what would cause undue anxiety, and this will help determine how much should be owned in stocks. Our age and income needs should also be incorporated but too many investors consider this first and minimize risk tolerance.

2. **What is your style? Aggressive? Income- oriented? Active with much trading or having long holding periods for**

investments? Make sure the manager or fund is meeting your objectives

This may be something that changes over time, and we may learn over time what fits us best. Also, as you age your objectives will change. At some point a growth style may evolve to wanting more income and stability depending on needs and objectives. The important thing is to be aware of what we are trying to accomplish and to merge those needs and objectives with our investments or our advisors.

3. **How diversified are the manager's investments?**

Many managers are more focused on fewer holdings than others. Be aware that being less diversified means more risk. However some managers may be too diversified. Some funds include every investment we can think of, including all types of fixed income, emerging market funds that may include countries we have never heard of, and other types of esoteric investments. My own philosophy is to stick with long-term investments that have historically provided solid returns. There is no reason to diversify and water down our portfolios with so many different holdings that we really don't even understand.

4. **What type of investments does your manager or your fund hold?**

Whether we have hired a manager or have a mutual fund, we should know what type of investments they will own, or we might risk being scared out when they invariably hit rough times. A manager will be willing to show a sample portfolio and the website Morningstar (www.morningstar.com) is a useful resource for funds—it lets you check most mutual funds or

ETFs, take a look at their performance, the allocation between sectors, and the top holdings. This way we can be confident of what the fund is holding and how much of the top holdings make up the fund. As an example, many tech fund ETFs hold up to 10% or more of the top tech names like Apple or Microsoft. To the degree that this fits our objective and these names do not dominate the other areas of our portfolio, this may be fine, but we should be aware before stepping in. At least by looking at the sector allocation and the top holdings we can get a feel for what the manager is emphasizing and how aggressive they might be.

5. **How have the investments performed?**

How has the manager performed in good environments and in bad? Most advisors can illustrate this, and mutual funds and websites such as Morningstar also share much of this information. It is human nature to favor the advisors who have recently performed the best, hence these are often the managers who have received the most inflows to their products and probably are the most popular. Be careful here and instead look at how a manager performs in different environments. For example, a strong long-term record might just be a function of several good years and many mediocre or down years. It is good to see year by year comparisons instead of just the long-term record. Also, did the manager perform great in up years but horribly in down years? Or vice versa? It isn't that one is better than another, but it can give us an idea of whether a manager fits our particular risk profile and objectives. As I mentioned, some would be put to sleep watching me manage money, but in bad years that means they can sleep at night because their risk is lessened. However, some are willing to take more risk or want a more active approach. All approaches can work but, ultimately, it's worth doing the homework to make sure a manager's philosophy fits your style.

6. **Be aware of the fees that you are paying.** Morningstar shows what each mutual fund or ETF is charging. These fees come out of the fund directly so if you don't look you may not ever know. Managers will tell you their fee but be sure they align with your expected long-term return. If you expect to earn 6% and the fee is 2%, then that is really subtracting substantially from your long-term expectations. Be sure the manager is upfront about all fees that are being charged and how much they might subtract from your total return.

CHAPTER 12

WHEN YOU'RE STEPPING INTO LIQUID, KEEP YOUR EYES ON DRY LAND

Survival Skills for Money Surfers Who Don't Have a Death Wish

One of the first real thrills of moving to San Diego and living the California dream was the joy of learning how to surf. To prepare together as a family, we watched a great documentary called *Stepping into Liquid,*[152] which highlighted the love of surfing from beginners to super surfers defying gravity, tossing and turning on the tops of impossibly huge waves. They seemed to make time stand still, and the physical laws of the universe were momentarily suspended. One surfer described it as one moment of joy, followed by another, and then another. It's living life fully, one second at a time.

My boys took to the ocean immediately and with such passion that they turned into California kids seemingly overnight. It's like they were born to it. Since the boys were now anatomically attached to their boards, it felt only natural that I should learn too. What fun, I thought, to have a lifetime sport that I could enjoy with them. Plus, surfing sounded very cool to me. I grew up in the landlocked Midwest. And anyway, surfing was something Elvis did in the movies.[153] Or Davy from the Monkees.[154] I was, as surfers say, stoked for the ride.

In the beginning, surfing was definitely cooler in theory than in practice. I stumbled and bumbled my way through my first classes. I remember the instructor having us practice standing up on the board while still on the beach. "It's just standing up," he would say, "you do this every day." Somehow, though, once we got into the ocean, with the waves coming at me and the board beginning to dance on the froth with increasing speed and buoyancy, nothing came naturally. Everything felt new and awkward. Like I was trying to stand on greased lightning. Where was my moment of joy? Where was my meditative experience when I felt at one with the universe?

I finally discovered that the key to standing up on my board was not in my feet, but in my eyes. I realized that when I looked down at the water, I followed my eyes right back into the drink. Once I started looking up, directing my focus toward the beach where I wanted to go, I stayed upright, and somehow, I got there. I got something else too. In those moments, balanced on my board, riding the waves, I felt the pure joy that my kids had felt immediately.

Chase the waves you're capable of riding

My boys were more devoted surfers than I, but now that I could at least string a few moments of surfer bliss together, I was happy to accommodate them. Almost every weekend we headed to the ocean. They would find a good spot where they knew they could catch the best waves, but of course that's where most other people were. I would usually wander down the beach a little, where there were fewer crowds. I was willing to settle for the waves that no one else wanted. I wasn't a connoisseur. I was just happy to remain vertical. But that's a big part of surfing—chasing the tasty waves can become a whole lifestyle.

One weekend my son suggested that we travel up the coast where there was supposedly one of the best surfing spots in California, a place called Trestles near San Clemente. We checked the surf report and the waves looked bigger than the ones we normally surfed but not impossible to manage, so we loaded the car and set off. The second we arrived the boys grabbed their boards and paddled out. I did my stretching, watching the surf closely. The waves definitely looked bigger than I had originally thought. I could see that the boys had made it out past the break safely, so I headed in after them.

Paddling out, I noticed that the waves weren't just bigger, there were also more of them. I kept diving under, the icy-cold water running down my wetsuit. The force of the breaks pounded me from all directions. I was losing my breath with every dive and there was no time to rest between the swells. I started to get tired. Then an even bigger set of waves rolled in. My son later told me that set was over 10 feet tall. Now, when I dove under, the wave had the power to hold me there. It occurred to me, at that moment, I might be drowning.

As I felt the panic start to rise in my throat, I looked over at another poor unfortunate fellow who had managed to get himself in over his head, just like me. Unlike me, though, this guy had kept his cool. He pointed to me, and then at the shore, reminding me to turn around and look at the beach, where I wanted to go, to let the next wave push me in toward the shore. It was such an easy fix. Why hadn't I thought of that? I turned around, the next wave pushed me in. My panic subsided and my brush with death was over as quickly as it had come upon me.

That memory of the ocean trying to swallow me up, that feeling of being in the grip of something larger than myself, came home in a different way just a few weeks later. I was heading to Dayton, Cincinnati, and finally Indianapolis to visit my clients and spend some time with my dad, who had tickets to the Bengals game. This was 2008, before the financial crash,[155] but things were starting to get bouncy. My dad and I chatted about the situation on the drive down to Cincinnati. Neither of us was terribly concerned. We were confident that Congress would pass a bailout package the next day, which would hold off a major decline. Our spirits were high, and we were able to enjoy some time together, without a care in the world.

It was a wonderful trip: quality time with my dad, warm and friendly meetings with my clients, a predictable and entirely typical Bengals loss. All was well. The next day, after another meeting, I drove to the airport, smiling and thinking about how wonderful it was to see successful clients and to be heading back home to see my kids—maybe even catch a few waves on the weekend. A few minutes after my arrival at Dayton International, however, everything changed. I had made it through security and had sat down to wait. I glanced up at the TV screen. What I saw instantly transported me to that place where the waves were overcoming me, and I felt like I was going to drown.

Apparently, at the last minute, Congress decided to vote against the bailout package.[156] The result was a shock to a market that was already teetering on the precipice. Now the genie would explode out of the bottle, and there was no way to put him back. The economy was in free fall, and it was anybody's guess what would happen next.

The market drop that day in September of 2008 is still one of the largest in history.[157] It dropped over 8%. Standing at my gate, I stared, mesmerized, as I watched it plummet. Then I called my dad. He had seen the news and was channeling my grandpa. He told me not to panic. He said that while it would be no picnic in the days ahead, it was probably best to put our heads in the sand for a few months and wait out the storm. My dad knew it would be impossible to ignore the biggest financial crash since the Great Depression,[158] but his advice was, as usual, sound and comforting, and we had the wiggle room to breathe. My dad was reminding me to look to the shore, to keep my eyes on the beach, and not look out to sea, where the swells were terrifying. He couldn't have been more right!

The next several months were the most volatile I have ever seen. It truly seemed like a wild ocean with great swelling peaks, plunging valleys, and a storm surge that was not to be believed. Older surfers have an expression I always liked, for when conditions are blown out of control like this. They call it "victory at sea,"[159] which refers to an old-World War II TV show that opened with a wild and stormy ocean. It did feel pretty bleak, just standing there and waiting for the global economy to crumble, but I kept remembering my dad's words, and I did not panic.

Over the course of the next three months, the market had six days where the daily move was over 7%: four of those were down, two of them down over 9%, and both exceeded the losses we experienced on that first day of panic. Two of the record days were actually up, and the up days were over 10%. Of course, in these cases they were mostly rebounding from the terrible down days. Between October of 2008 and March of 2009, the S&P 500 dropped a full 46%.[160]

There was more than enough blame to go around. Here are just a few of the missteps we made in the years previous:

1. The unwinding of Depression-era regulations like Glass–Steagall[161] that had been put in place to avoid catastrophes like this.

2. The genius idea of allowing investment banks to package mortgages and sell off low-quality loans in bundles that few understood, except for the bankers who sold the junk to their investors.[162]

3. Sloppy mortgage companies encouraging homebuyers to buy homes with little or no money down and with an adjustable-rate mortgage that could overwhelm the buyer if the rates rose.

4. Overly optimistic homebuyers, who failed to imagine what might happen if their adjustable-rate mortgage went up or they lost their job.

5. Investors who could see Lehman and other banks going under but believed things would just work out.[163]

6. A perennially adolescent Congress, who failed to recognize that during a crisis they had to grow up and be leaders.

7. Every recent President who did not step in and acknowledge the damage that our excess was doing to the economy.

In the end, most of us could look in the mirror and find at least a couple of bad decisions that had come back to haunt us. But pointing the finger or playing the blame game doesn't help in a crisis. It may make you feel better momentarily, but it doesn't address the problem. The only thing that will help is time, and not making the same mistakes twice. And though we wish bankers and politicians were always looking out for our best interests, often they are as unemotional and as uncaring as the ocean, so you better be able to control your own surfboard and get yourself to shore.

Given the devastation in the markets in 2008, it is odd to say that in some respects it was the most gratifying time in my career. It wasn't that I had predicted this disaster like those fellows in the movie *The Big Short*.[164] And it wasn't because I smiled like a peaceful Buddha while the Titanic sank. My stomach was in a perpetual knot. What was rewarding was that all the safeguards I had learned over the years, the cautious approach that had been instilled in me from my grandpa to my uncle and my dad, had been tested. And in the face of that victory-at-sea-scale disaster, my clients', and my own funds, held together quite well.

When you can't be safe, at least be careful

Many folks asked me then and since if I was constantly on the phone with scared clients during the crash of 2008. In fact, I did hear from clients, but they were calling because they were worried about me, not themselves. They were concerned that I was emotionally upset over the chaos. They knew their money was secure, and because they were relaxed about their own situation, they could take time to be concerned about me and show me kindness in the middle of a crash.

I had already reduced stocks that had seemed risky, because the trends had crossed thresholds that I had set to sell if they crossed. The bond market was in disarray if investors had bought risky bonds, but my philosophy was to never take risks with safe money and treasury bonds actually made money during this time. And since I was constantly making sure that allocations were not out of line with objectives, no one had more stocks than they could afford or that would cause them to lose sleep at night.

As chaotic as the world had become, my clients' financial lives were relatively stable. One might argue that by being so conservative they were missing the thrill of riding the 10-footers, but what I saw was them surviving a stormy sea because they had been measured and disciplined. They could hold on through the crisis by not losing more than what would cause them to panic and, ultimately, they were able to catch great values as we could pick off stocks at lower prices.

Inspiring Words You Can Take to the Bank

You can't always get what you want but if you try sometimes, you get what you need.[165]
—ROLLING STONES

Muddy water is best cleared by leaving it alone.[166]
—ALAN WATTS

The best way to measure your investing success is not by whether you're beating the market but by whether you've put in place a financial plan and a behavioral discipline that are likely to get you where you want to go.[167]
—BENJAMIN GRAHAM

The golden rules still apply

Even though I may have felt like I was drowning during the crash, the truth is, I wasn't. I had been prepared, and so were my clients, not because I had some magical second sight that allowed me to predict what was coming, but because I followed some tried and true rules that really aren't all that complicated. In a way, it all goes back to what they tried to teach us as kids in those golden days of yore. Be sensible. Don't get out over your surfboard. Put some money aside for a rainy day.

Ironically, the embodiment of this advice came in the form of a schoolteacher named Betsy who was one of my clients and a great example of what exemplifies the ideal investor. In fact, I visited her just before that fateful trip to the airport before the panic. The way Betsy handles her finances is like a trip back to the fundamental values that built the American Dream.

Betsy's mom grew up during the Depression. The family had been forced to leave their home when her father lost everything. Although he did eventually recover and became quite successful in the car business, the experience left a mark on his daughter and granddaughter—they would always thereafter be prepared for the rug to be pulled out from under them. Betsy's mom had a habit of setting aside a few coins out of every paycheck and rolling them up in coin wrappers to add to their savings.

Even as a little girl, Betsy adopted the very same habit of putting something aside for a rainy day. She was given an allowance, school lunch money, and bus fare, and yet from this bare-bones budget, Betsy always managed to squirrel a little bit away. This good savings hygiene continued into her adult life. Betsy traveled and lived a nice life, but she always made sure she could afford what she bought and that there was a little extra left over, in case things got gnarly.

Although her grandfather had lost most of his money in the stock market during the Depression, when he was back to making money, he went right back to buying stocks. This time, though, he was in for the long term. He gave Betsy a few shares of stock and told her to hold on to them, to not worry about short-term fluctuations, because over the long term these were conservative stocks that would perform well. Sound familiar?

Betsy always lived within her means and did not over-extend. She rented an apartment for a long time in order to save up for a down payment on a house. She wanted to be sure that her mortgage payment was not too high and when she finally had enough saved up, she bought a house she could afford. Each year she would add one additional monthly mortgage payment to her principal and with the help of a refinance, eventually paid off what was originally a 30-year mortgage in just eight years. Even though her home is now paid off, Betsy still pays the same monthly amount that she owed in her mortgage, only now it's to herself into an account that she calls her "house fund." With this fund she has added a deck and refinished her kitchen. Betsy has no need for a home equity loan—she is her own bank.

Over time, Betsy added to her grandfather's stocks. She would occasionally buy a few more shares of the ones she already held. Sometimes her uncle would suggest a stock that he felt had long-term potential. What had started as just a few thousand dollars began to grow, and all the while, Betsy just continued to build and save. In the early 1990s, by which time she had slowly and methodically accumulated over $600,000, she decided that an investment advisor might help over the long term. She hired me.

We kept her conservative approach. We combined stocks that I recommended with her original portfolio and found a good balance between stocks and bonds to make sure that any extreme volatility would not jeopardize the savings and investment that she had so carefully and skillfully built over the years. By the time we had that meeting just before the 2008 decline, her account had a value of over $2 million.

As I mentioned, I did not predict the crash of 2008. I made no great prognostication in my meeting with Betsy right before the market plunged. Despite the volatility that preceded the crash, I told her I thought it best to stick to the target allocation that best met her long-term objectives. We had recently sold a few stocks to get back to that target and I mentioned there was a possibility of a correction as the Fed had raised interest rates, and bond yields were higher. I assured her that we had enough in reserves to withstand any potential weakness.

Betsy was pleased with how her account had grown, understood the conservative balance, had seen ups and downs over the years, and believed in long-term investing. She had her grandfather's patience. She accepted that things might weaken some but was confident in our strategy and discipline. As always, at the end of the meeting she thanked me for my guidance and told me she appreciated all I had done to keep her account growing. I smiled, as always, and told her she had done all the hard work, because she had saved, lived within her means, and stuck with a long-term strategy. The meeting was, as always, a mutual admiration society.

Typically, that would have been our last conversation for a few months. Instead, we spoke the very next day to share our shock over how things had changed and how it might affect her portfolio. "Mick," she said, "I know my money is fine, I'm not worried. You always warned me these things will happen, that markets go up and down, and so I know we were prepared. I just hope you are okay, because I know that I am."

Betsy survived the crash of 2008 because she had done everything right. So I thought, nearing the end of this book, I would share her simple, yet tried and true method for mellowing money.

Betsy's Method for Achieving Financial Security Even When the Bottom Falls Out

1. First and foremost, Betsy always saved a little money. I believe too many people underestimate this simple exercise. Savings will typically outperform investments, especially in the early years. Betsy began saving as a child and when she started working, she did what too many don't—when her paycheck arrived, she paid herself (her savings) first.

2. Betsy took a long view on stocks. She bought companies that she could hold on to and watch grow.

3. Betsy knew her risk tolerance and realized what level of investment she could tolerate if things went haywire, as they did in 2008. This kept her in a calm state whether the waves were small and the water smooth and glassy, or the ocean was

churning and the waves were building into a "victory at sea."

4. Thanks to her grandfather, Betsy understood that if you are going to step into liquid, you can't avoid the occasional wild ride. It's just the motion of the ocean. You can't prepare for a crisis in the midst of a crisis, so make sure you are ready before you even step into the water.

I still surf with my boys and now even my young daughter joins in. I use a foam board, which isn't very cool-looking, but I know it won't put me in the hospital if it smacks me in the head. I don't paddle out on "victory-at-sea" days—I know my limitations and I check the surf report before I get in the water. This way I can experience those great moments of joy, whether I'm standing up on my board and riding a tasty wave or just sitting peacefully in still water, waiting for a wave to happen.

The lessons I learned from surfing didn't kill me, but they almost did. The lessons we learn in the market are similar in many ways, and sometimes feel just as deadly. So often when we step into liquid, we focus on that short-term thrill, the stoke of riding the crest of a huge wave all the way to the beach, even though we know that getting into deep water has the potential to drown us.

Fun family surfing

Tips for Surfing in a Victory-At-Sea Market

1. **Prepare for nature's unpredictability before entering the water:** I'm not suggesting that we minimize the thrill of the crest—by all means, revel in the joy of life's peak moments—but understand that the market has the capability to pull us under. Though volatile markets may make us feel panicky, we won't have to be terrified of drowning if we've already prepared for the possibility of market turmoil.

2. **Look to the shore, not down into the drink:** In surfing we go where our eyes are looking and if we look down that's often where we will go. In the markets we can also become drawn away from what we want to achieve. Headlines, politics, pandemics, economic announcements, and wars can cause us to lose our focus, can distract us from the long-term trend of the market and our long-term objectives.

3. **Don't be afraid to just stay still and take in the beauty of the ocean:** The moments of joy in surfing are dwarfed by the moments of sitting in the water. So too are the moments in the market. Often it is best to sit and not make big decisions. Moments of turmoil usually end quickly. Even the 2008 financial crisis was mostly over for investors within six months. The decline during the pandemic was mostly over within three weeks. However, even during moments of calm, surfers are still reading the ocean. Then, when the wave comes, they are prepared. The time for action in the markets is also during times of calm, and when moments of turmoil come, sometimes for investors it is best to just sit.

EPILOGUE

Pay No Attention to the Man
Behind the Curtain

When I was growing up in Dayton, my dad did a lot of business in Cincinnati and so his law firm gave him a special phone that could dial direct to Cincinnati from Dayton at no charge. It was called a WATS (Wide Area Telephone Service) line[168] and I thought it was just about the most amazing invention since string cheese. I realize that this sounds a little ridiculous to those of us today who can call China for no additional charge, but back in the day, the WATS line was the coolest thing going. The phone was bright red, and it sat front and center in our TV room. My sisters and I called it the Bat Phone.[169]

One night we were watching the Cincinnati Reds, back when they actually won games, but this night they had been trailing the whole game until the 9th inning. Then, suddenly, they came alive and with two outs, Ken Griffey Sr.[170] hit a line shot over the wall to win the game. My friend and I were ecstatic, jumping up and down, giving high fives, and then we both looked at that red phone and had the same thought: "Let's call Ken Griffey on the Bat Phone!"

We called Cincinnati information, and the operator gave us the number for Riverfront Stadium. We dialed the number but neither of us really thought there was any chance Ken Griffey would pick up. But why not give it a shot? When the stadium's operator picked up, we asked to speak to Ken Griffey. She told us to hold. And we did. We held our breath, waiting to see what would happen. Then we heard a deep voice come on the other end. "Hello?" it said, and we froze. Then my excitement got the best of me.

"Ken, that was a great hit!" I said so loudly I probably dented his eardrum. My friend and I looked at each other expecting the baseball star to hang up on us once he realized he had a couple of crazy kids on the other end of the line. Then I had an idea. "We are Tom and Mick, and we're the leaders of the Ken Griffey fan club. We just wanted to tell you we think you are the best player on the team."

Full transparency: there was no Ken Griffey fan club in Dayton. Or at least, there wasn't until that very moment, and we were the only members. Ken laughed and thanked us and told us how happy and proud he was to have a fan club and to talk to its two co-presidents. We went to school the next day 10 feet taller than the day before.

That Bat Phone and our brief conversation with Ken Griffey earned us major street cred with the kids. Before we knew it, we had started a Ken Griffey fan club for real and often tried to get Ken and his wife to meet us after games so we could shake his hand. This never happened, but it didn't matter. We were almost celebrities ourselves thanks to our chance encounter with a legend. We had been close to greatness, so we were proximal heroes. Hero worship seems to be part of our culture and certainly doesn't disappear as we age.

Years later I met another star, this time it was a star trader at a technical analysis conference. At the time, I was beginning to think that the path of long-term investing might be too boring. Maybe my future wasn't in analysis after all, maybe I belonged on the floor. So I was anxious to hear what this trader had to say. He had led the Chicago Board of Trade with his profits that year, earning over $30 million in returns.

He was charismatic, full of good humor, and stood out as a star at the conference. He immediately pulled us all in with his stories and eventually his methods. As he was nearing the end of his talk, he told us in a conspiratorial whisper that he would now reveal exactly what he did to make his money—his exact trading methodology. We were on the edge of our seats. This was it, we thought, this was our shot at stardom.

He prefaced his remarks by saying that although he would share his secret, none of us would be able to copy his system. He challenged each of us to try to copy it and come back in a year to show him that he was wrong. I along with the other 30 attendees only smiled thinking, *challenge accepted!*

What was his big celebrity secret? Okay, here it comes. In short, he ran his portfolio by expecting to lose a small amount of money 90% of the time and letting the remaining 10% of big wins wipe out the small losses and then some. In other words, you had to be able to endure 90% of your bets being bad bets in order to have a shot at the big gain, the gain that would potentially make you a star trader.

The speaker explained how his system was almost foolproof, except for the psychological part, a caveat we all of course ignored. Surely any trade only had five possibilities: small loss, big loss, no gain, small gain, or big gain. What was eliminated in his system were big losses, but in order do this he had to take an infinite number of small losses. In fact, anytime a trade moved against him, he was out of it. He was only willing to hold on to winners, and these occasional big wins made him a star on the trading floor and very, very rich!

As you can tell if you've made it this far in my writing, the title of the book is not *How to Make Millions by Trading*. I'm quite sure that there are countless methods, articles, and trading tools out there for you if that is your desire. And I still believe the method that I learned from the star trader many years ago actually works. But it didn't work for me! Imagine losing trade after trade, sometimes 30 in a row, before that big win. I not only imagined it, I did it, but I couldn't take it and I never got to the big wins. I did not have the confidence to keep taking the losses.

I would always rationalize that I should hold on and wait, that eventually the trade would work out. But it would keep sliding. Then I would look at that loss and rationalize, well I'll hold on to that one for the long term. There's an old joke about traders—the long-term investments are the losers that you just didn't want to sell. This was why the star trader so happily challenged us to try but believed we would fail. He knew that most young traders would not have the confidence or personality make-up to keep to the discipline.

He was sure right about me. Yes, I had met a star but learned in a costly way that just because he had found his way, it wasn't necessarily and likely would not be mine. I had to find my own path and though taking the long-run view might be like "watching paint dry" compared to the excitement of the trading floor, it happened to be my path to success, though I may not have realized it for many years.

There is no place like home

Years ago, Alan Greenspan was the head of the Federal Reserve and if there ever was a wizard, I thought it was surely him. He was brilliant and, in many ways, beautifully guided the economy in the 1990s and early 2000s. But he was human. As mentioned earlier, one of the statements he is known for is calling the stock market valuation at the time an example of "irrational exuberance." The afternoon that he said this, the markets around the world fell, though not for very long. Soon they began their continued uptrend. In fact, he said this in 1996, over three years before the market experienced any significant decline. He may have been a studied and accomplished economist but in predicting the future of the markets his crystal ball was as cloudy as the rest of ours.

I remember thinking of *The Wizard of Oz* when the Wizard barks, "Pay no attention to that man behind the curtain!" Naturally, he wanted Dorothy and her friends to believe he was bigger, greater, and more powerful than just one old man from Kansas. Most of us really do want to believe in wizards, but they never turn out to be wizards at all, just another guy behind the curtain who lost his way in a hot air balloon on his way to the county fair. A famous 9th-century Buddhist monk, Li Yixian, once reportedly told his students, "If you meet the Buddha on the road, kill him."

Obviously, he was not talking about pulling out an Uzi. And certainly, there are many interpretations out there, but for me it always resonated with questioning any outside force or person or thoughts that did not resonate with my own true feelings and nature. In other words, too often we see others as the Wizard, when we should look to ourselves to find our way home.

As I matured as an investor, I came to understand that I had the answers already, inside myself, waiting for challenging experiences to reveal their deeper meaning. Many of those challenges and lessons I have related here in this book. I hope you take what I say with the sincerity with which I have offered it—and also with a grain of salt. Find your own way, both in life and in the market, learn from the lessons of experience, and perhaps most importantly of all, enjoy the ride.

THE END

To keep in touch, visit me at
www.mellowyourmoney.com

ENDNOTES

1   James Grant, "Louis Rukeyser, Television Host, Dies at 73," May 3, 2006, https://www.nytimes.com/2006/05/03/business/media/03rukeyser.html.

2   *Orson Welles*, IMDb online, accessed October 17, 2022, https://www.imdb.com/name/nm0000080/?ref_=nv_sr_srsg_0.

3   *Dead Poets Society*, IMDb online, accessed October 17, 2022, https://www.imdb.com/title/tt0097165/?ref_=nv_sr_srsg_0.

4   *Stand and Deliver*, IMDb online, accessed October 17, 2022, https://www.imdb.com/title/tt0094027/?ref_=nv_sr_srsg_0.

5   *School of Rock*, IMDb online, accessed October 17, 2022, https://www.imdb.com/title/tt0332379/?ref_=nv_sr_srsg_0.

6   "Procter & Gamble – 52 Year Stock Price History," *Microtrends* online, accessed October 17, 2022, https://www.macrotrends.net/stocks/charts/PG/procter-gamble/stock-price-history.

7   "Johnson & Johnson – 52 Year Stock Price History," *Microtrends* online, accessed October 17, 2022, https://www.macrotrends.net/stocks/charts/JNJ/johnson-johnson/stock-price-history.

8   "McDonald's – 52 Year Stock Price History," *Microtrends* online, accessed October 17, 2022, https://www.macrotrends.net/stocks/charts/MCD/mcdonalds/stock-price-history.

9   "Colgate-Palmolive – 45 Year Stock Price History" *Microtrends* online, accessed October 17, 2022, https://www.macrotrends.net/stocks/charts/CL/colgate-palmolive/stock-price-history.

10   Edwin Lefèvre, *Reminiscences of a Stock Operator* (George H. Doran Company, 1923), https://www.trendfollowing.com/whitepaper/Edwin_LeFevre_Reminiscences_of_a_Stock_Operator.pdf.

11   Amy, "Misquotes and Misattribution," *Lost in a Good Book* website, October 25, 2016, https://lostinagoodbk.com/2016/10/25/misquotes-and-misattribution/.

12   Gilbert K. Chesterton, "AZ Quotes," last modified October 17, 2022, https://www.azquotes.com/quote/607924.

13   "George Norlin," University of Colorado Boulder online, accessed October 17, 2022, https://www.colorado.edu/libraries/about/history/george-norlin.

14   Shah Gilani, "The Four Most Dangerous Words in Investing," MarketWatch online, last modified March 1, 2011, https://www.marketwatch.com/story/four-most-dangerous-words-in-investing-2011-03-01.

15   "Michael Crichton: Quotes," accessed October 17, 2022, https://www.goodreads.com/quotes/188569-if-you-don-t-know-history-then-you-don-t-know-anything.

16   "Investors Beware: Markets Could Still Head Lower," *Barron's* online, last modified March 30, 2020, https://www.barrons.com/magazine/20200330

17   "Here's How the Market Reacted to the Attack on Pearl Harbor 75 Years Ago," *Benzinga* online, December 7, 2016, https://www.benzinga.com/general/education/16/12/8780102/heres-how-the-market-reacted-to-the-attack-on-pearl-harbor-75-years.

18   "Great Depression: Facts and Related Content," *Britannica* **online**, accessed October 17, 2022, https://www.britannica.com/facts/Great-Depression.

19   John Spacey, "3 Origins of This Too Shall Pass," Simplicable website, last modified October 26, 2019, https://simplicable.com/new/this-too-shall-pass.

20   *The Great Gatsby*, (1974) IMDb online, accessed October 17, 2022, https://www.imdb.com/title/tt0071577/?ref_=nv_sr_srsg_3.

21   *The Great Gatsby*, (2013) IMDb online, accessed October 17, 2022, https://www.imdb.com/title/tt1343092/?ref_=hm_rvi_tt_i_3.

22   *Seabiscuit*, IMDb online, accessed October 17, 2022, https://www.imdb.com/title/tt0329575/?ref_=nv_sr_srsg_0.

23   "Of Mice and Men," *IMDb* online, accessed October 17, 2022, https://www.imdb.com/title/tt0105046/?ref_=fn_al_tt_0. George and Lennie are not brothers. George identifies Lennie as his cousin at one point, but it's clearly a cover story—they are not related in any way. https://www.enotes.com/homework-help/mice-men-what-lennie-george-662947.

24   "Chief Seattle's Farewell Speech," Native History-Native Experiences-Native Voices of First Nations Peoples, accessed October 17, 2022, https://firstpeoplesvoices.com/seattle.htm.

25   "Ponca Chief White Eagle: Be Still…Then Act…," *Stillness Speaks* online, accessed October 17, 2022, https://www.stillnessspeaks.com/ponca-white-eagle-still-act/.

26   "Chief Seattle: Quotes," *Goodreads* online, accessed October 17, 2022, https://www.goodreads.com/quotes/7362241-humankind-has-not-woven-the-web-of-life-we-are.

27   "Fyodor Dostoevsky: Quotes," *Goodreads* online, accessed October 17, 2022, https://www.goodreads.com/quotes/326879-drive-nature-out-of-the-door-and-it-will-fly.

28   Deborah C. Sawyer, "Dome Petroleum Limited," last modified July 16, 2014, https://www.thecanadianencyclopedia.ca/en/article/dome-petroleum-limited.

29   "A Review of Past Recessions," *Investopedia* online, last modified July 16, 2022, https://www.investopedia.com/articles/economics/08/past-recessions.asp; David Wessel, "What We Learned from Reagan's Tax Cuts," *Brookings* online, last modified December 8, 2017, https://www.brookings.edu/blog/up-front/2017/12/08/what-we-learned-from-reagans-tax-cuts/; "Reagan Signs Economic Recovery Tax Act," *History* online, last modified August 11, 2021, https://www.history.com/this-day-in-history/reagan-signs-economic-recovery-tax-act-erta.; Joseph Thorndike, "Reagan's Tax Cut Just Turned 40…," *Forbes* online, last modified September 3. 2021, https://www.forbes.com/sites/taxnotes/2021/09/03/reagans-tax-cut-just-turned-40---and-its-still-the-most-important-tax-reform-since-world-war-ii/?sh=1357f3675d14.; Nicole Lewis, "Did Ronald Reagan's 1981 Tax Cut Supercharge the Economy?", *The Washington Post* online, last modified November 8, 2017, https://www.washingtonpost.com/news/fact-checker/wp/2017/11/08/did-ronald-reagans-1981-tax-cut-supercharge-the-economy/.

30   "Dow Industrials: 1981-1982 Bear Market," accessed October 17, 2022, *Fiend's Bear Encounters Page* online, http://www.fiendbear.com/bear1981.htm; Tom Petruno, "A Look Back at a Great Bull Market," *LA Times* online, last modified August 13, 2002, https://www.latimes.com/archives/la-xpm-2002-aug-13-fi-bull13-story.html.

31   Frank W. Slusser, "Stocks Score Best Gain in 7 Years on Record Volume in Historic 1982," last modified December 31, 1982, https://www.upi.com/Archives/1982/12/31/Stocks-score-best-gain-in-7-years-on-record-volume-in-historic-1982/6401410158800/.

32   *The Wolf of Wall Street*, IMDb online, accessed October 17, 2022, https://www.imdb.com/title/tt0993846/?ref_=nv_sr_srsg_0.

33   "Brief History," *OPEC* online, accessed October 17, 2022, https://www.opec.org/opec_web/en/about_us/24.htm.

34   "Timeline: Gold's Steady Rise to a Glittering $1,000 an Ounce," *Reuters* online, last updated September 7, 2009, https://www.reuters.com/article/us-markets-precious-timeline-sb/timeline-golds-steady-rise-to-a-glittering-1000-an-ounce-idUSTRE58708520090908.

35   Tyler Crowe, "The 1980s Just Called—It Thinks You Should Buy Oil Stocks," last modified December 21, 2014, https://www.fool.com/investing/general/2014/12/21/1980s-just-called-thinks-buy-big-oil-stocks.aspx.

36   Sam Mattera, "IBM Used to be Bigger than Apple, What Happened?", *Nasdaq* online, April 11, 2015, https://www.nasdaq.com/articles/ibm-used-be-bigger-apple-what-happened-2015-04-11.

37   Brian Kachejian, "The History of Woolworth's," accessed October 17, 2022, https://classicnewyorkhistory.com/the-history-of-woolworths/.

38   "Eastman Kodak Company," *Britannica* **online**, last modified September 22, 2022, https://www.britannica.com/topic/Eastman-Kodak-Company.

39   Deborah C. Sawyer, "Dome Petroleum Limited," last modified July 16, 2014, https://www.thecanadianencyclopedia.ca/en/article/dome-petroleum-limited.

40   "Charles MacKey: Quotes," *Goodreads* online, accessed October 17, 2022, https://www.goodreads.com/quotes/289693-men-it-has-been-well-said-think-in-herds-it.

41   "Michel de Montaigne: Quotes," *Goodreads* online, accessed October 17, 2022, https://www.goodreads.com/quotes/6751782-my-life-has-been-full-of-terrible-misfortunes-most-of

42   *AZ Quotes* online, accessed October 17, 2022, https://www.azquotes.com/quote/773019 (Includes internal citation for original source.)

43   "Stock Market Crash of 1987," *Investopedia* online, January 22, 2021, https://www.investopedia.com/terms/s/stock-market-crash-1987.asp.; Donald Bernhardt and Marshall Eckblad, "Stock Market Crash of 1987," last modified November 22, 2013, https://www.federalreservehistory.org/essays/stock-market-crash-of-1987.; "The Black Monday Stock Market Crash," *Library of Congress* online, accessed October 17, 2022, https://guides.loc.gov/this-month-in-business-history/october/black-monday-stock-market-crash.

44   "Alan Watts," *Famous Philosophers* online, accessed October 17, 2022, https://www.famousphilosophers.org/alan-watts/. Allan Watts was an influential philosopher who gave lectures at universities across the United States.

45   Joshua Horn, "The Great Dayton Flood of 1913," last modified March 25, 2013, https://discerninghistory.com/2013/03/the-great-dayton-flood/.; Lisa Powell, "The Great Dayton Flood of 1913…," last modified March 24, 2013, https://www.daytondailynews.com/news/the-great-dayton-flood-1913-things-know-about-broken-levees-rescue-boats-and-lost-lives/6MzhsTtAysABc4pFACBjpL/.; "Dayton Homes Damaged by the 1913 Flood Photographs," Ohio Memory Collection, https://ohiomemory.org/digital/collection/p267401coll36/id/5293/.; "Value of $100,000,000 from 1913 to 2022," CPI Inflation Calculator, https://www.in2013dollars.com/us/inflation/1913?amount=100000000.

46   Walter A. Friedman, "John H. Patterson and the Sales Strategy of the National Cash Register Company, 1884 to 1922," last modified November 1, 1999, https://hbswk.hbs.edu/item/john-h-patterson-and-the-sales-strategy-of-the-national-cash-register-company-1884-to-1922.

47   "Charles K. Kettering," *Britannica* **online**, accessed October 17, 2022, https://www.britannica.com/biography/Charles-F-Kettering.

48   "The Stock Market Crash of 1929," ER Services, accessed October 17, 2022, https://courses.lumenlearning.com/suny-ushistory2os2xmaster/chapter/the-stock-market-crash-of-1929/; "Great Depression," Ohio History Central, accessed October 17, 2022, https://ohiohistorycentral.org/w/Great_Depression.; Thomas Schwartz, "The Great Stock Market of 1929: Why History Textbooks and the Conventional Wisdom Get It Wrong," National Archives Hoover Heads, last modified June 15, 2022, https://hoover.blogs.archives.gov/2022/06/15/the-great-stock-market-crash-of-1929-why-history-textbooks-and-the-conventional-wisdom-get-it-wrong/.

49   "A History of Credit Scores: When Did They Become a Thing?", *Point* online, January 26, 2022, https://www.point.app/article/a-history-of-credit-scores-when-did-they-become-a-thing.; Victoria Araj, "A History of Credit," Rocket HQ, last modified December 22, 2021, https://www.rockethq.com/learn/credit/the-history-of-credit.; Krista Reese, "Equifax," last modified August 19, 2013, New Georgia Encyclopedia, https://www.georgiaencyclopedia.org/articles/business-economy/equifax/.

50   Brian Duignan, "Causes of the Great Depression," *Britannica* online, accessed October 17, 2022, https://www.britannica.com/story/causes-of-the-great-depression.

51   *Wall Street*, IMDb online, accessed October 17, 2022, https://www.imdb.com/title/tt0094291/?ref_=nv_sr_srsg_3.

52   *The Wolf of Wall Street*, *IMDb* online, accessed October 17, 2022, https://www.imdb.com/title/tt0993846/?ref_=nv_sr_srsg_0.

53   *The Bonfire of the Vanities*, IMDb online, accessed October 17, 2022, https://www.imdb.com/title/tt0099165/?ref_=nv_sr_srsg_0.

54   "Wisdom of Great Investors," *Davis Funds* online, accessed October 17, 2022, https://davisfunds.com/wisdom/quotes.php.

55   Jeremy Blatch, "An Expensive Place to Find Out Who You Are," SUR in English, last modified March 19, 2021, https://www.surinenglish.com/opinion/202103/19/expensive-place-find-20210319100135-v.html.

56   "Isaac Newton > Quotes," *Goodreads* online, accessed October 17, 2022, https://www.goodreads.com/quotes/74548-i-can-calculate-the-motion-of-heavenly-bodies-but-not.

57   "Success Is Never Final and Failure Never Fatal. It's Courage that Counts," Quote Investigator, accessed October 17, 2022, https://quoteinvestigator.com/2013/09/03/success-final/.

58   "What Is a Savings and Loan (S&L)?", *Bankrate* online, accessed October 17, 2022, https://www.bankrate.com/mortgages/savings-and-loan-associations/.

59   Kenneth J. Robinson, "Savings and Loan Crisis," Federal Reserve History, last modified November 22, 2013, https://www.federalreservehistory.org/essays/savings-and-loan-crisis.; Robert J. Samuelson, "Decade of Greed II," *The Washington Post online*, last modified July 14, 1999, https://www.washingtonpost.com/archive/opinions/1999/07/14/decade-of-greed-ii/fe36428e-a930-47f0-953e-84c940cada24/.

60   Greg Griffin, "Silverado Collapse Cost Taxpayers $1 Billion," *The Denver Post* online last modified May 7, 2016, https://www.denverpost.com/2008/09/29/silverado-collapse-cost-taxpayers-1-billion/.; Peter Carlson, "The Relatively Charmed Life of Neil Bush," *The Washington Post* online, last modified December 28, 2003, https://www.washingtonpost.com/archive/lifestyle/2003/12/28/the-relatively-charmed-life-of-neil-bush/388db316-f6b9-456e-8720-b4b2bf60a8ab/.; Henry David Rosso, "Neil Bush, Others Settle Silverado Lawsuit for $49.5 Million," UPI, last modified May 30, 1991, https://www.upi.com/Archives/1991/05/30/Neil-Bush-others-settle-Silverado-lawsuit-for-495-million/2631675576000/.

61   Dennis Lythgoe, "A Decade of Excess and Escape," Deseret News online, last
      modified December 31, 1989, https://www.deseret.com/1989/12/31/18839048/a-
      decade-of-excess-and-escape.; Robert J. Samuelson, "Decade of Greed II," *The
      Washington Post* online, last modified July 14, 1999, https://www.washingtonpost.
      com/archive/opinions/1999/07/14/decade-of-greed-ii/fe36428e-a930-47f0-953e-
      84c940cada24/.

62   Donald J. Trump with Tony Schwartz, *Trump: The Art of the Deal*, (Ballantine
      Books, New York, 2015), https://www.amazon.com/Trump-Art-Deal-Donald-J/
      dp/0399594493.

63   "Savings and Loan Association," *Britannica* online, accessed October 17, 2022,
      https://www.britannica.com/topic/savings-and-loan-association.

64   "Savings and Loan Industry (U.S.)," Economic History Association, accessed October
      17, 2022, https://eh.net/encyclopedia/savings-and-loan-industry-u-s/.

65   Will Kenton, "Savings and Loan (S&L) Crisis," Investopedia, last modified July 30,
      2021, https://www.investopedia.com/terms/s/sl-crisis.asp.

66   Kenneth J. Robinson, "Savings and Loan Crisis," Federal Reserve History, last
      modified November 22, 2013, https://www.federalreservehistory.org/essays/savings-
      and-loan-crisis.

67   Bert Ely, "Savings and Loan Crisis," *Econlib* online, accessed October 17, 2022,
      https://www.econlib.org/library/Enc/SavingsandLoanCrisis.html.

68   "The Economic Effects of the Savings & Loan Crisis," Congressional Budget Office
      online, accessed October 17, 2022, https://www.cbo.gov/sites/default/files/102nd-
      congress-1991-1992/reports/1992_01_theeconeffectsofthesavings.pdf.

69   *It's a Wonderful Life*, IMDb online, accessed October 17, 2022, https://www.imdb.
      com/title/tt0038650/?ref_=nv_sr_srsg_0.

70   *American Hustle*, IMDb online, accessed October 17, 2022, https://www.imdb.com/
      title/tt1800241/?ref_=nv_sr_srsg_0.

71   *Swimming with Sharks*, IMDb online, accessed October 17, 2022, https://www.imdb.
      com/title/tt0114594/?ref_=nv_sr_srsg_2.

72   "A Bull Market Is Like Sex," *Buffet Quotes* online, accessed October 17, 2022, https://
      buffettquotes.com/a-bull-market-is-like-sex/.

73   "Sigmund Freud: Quotes," *Goodreads* online, accessed October 17, 2022, https://
      www.goodreads.com/quotes/88666-illusions-commend-themselves-to-us-because-
      they-save-us-pain.

74   "Fyodor Dostoevsky: Quotes," *Goodreads* online, accessed October 17, 2022, https://
      www.goodreads.com/quotes/388563-through-error-you-come-to-the-truth-i-am-a.

75   James Doubek, "50 Years Ago, the Munich Olympics Massacre Changed How We
      Think About Terrorism," NPR, last modified September 4, 2022, https://www.npr.
      org/2022/09/04/1116641214/munich-olympics-massacre-hostage-terrorism-israel-
      germany.

76   "Stocks Then and Now: The 1950s and 1970s," *Investopedia* online, January 26, 2021, https://www.investopedia.com/articles/stocks/09/stocks-1950s-1970s.asp.

77   "Questions and Answers…," Department of the Treasury online, accessed October 17, 2022, https://treasurydirect.gov/forms/savpdp0035.pdf; "30 Year Treasure Rate – 39 Year Historical Chart," Macrotrends, accessed October 17, 2022, https://www.macrotrends.net/2521/30-year-treasury-bond-rate-yield-chart.; "Treasure Notes & Bonds History," Treasure Direct, accessed October 17, 2022, https://treasurydirect.gov/auctions/notes-and-bonds-history/.

78   Brenda Richardson, "How Low Are Mortgage Rates Right Now? Just Look at the Sky-High Numbers from the '80s and '90s," Money, last modified July 21, 2020, https://money.com/how-low-are-mortgage-rates-right-now-just-look-at-the-sky-high-numbers-from-the-80s-and-90s/.; Denny Ceizyk, "Historical Mortgage Rates: Averages Trends from the 1970s to 2022," Value Penguin, last modified October 21, 2022, https://www.valuepenguin.com/mortgages/historical-mortgage-rates.

79   "'Certificates of Confiscation' Part II," *PennMutual* online, April 18, 2022, https://www.pennmutualam.com/market-insights-news/blogs/monday-morning-perspectives/2022-04-18-revisiting-certificates-of-confiscation-part-ii.

80   Mikala Lugen, "The Day Disco Died: Remembering the Unbridled Chaos of 'Disco Demolition Night'", edm.com, last modified July 12, 2021, https://edm.com/features/remembering-disco-demolition-night-1979.

81   "The 1980 U.S. Olympic Team," U.S. Hockey Hall of Fame, accessed October 17, 2022, https://www.ushockeyhalloffame.com/page/show/831562-the-1980-u-s-olympic-team.

82   "Al Michaels," *NBC Sports* online, accessed October 17, 2022, https://nbcsportsgrouppressbox.com/bio/al-michaels/.

83   James Chen, "Who Is Peter Lynch," Investopedia, last modified August 18, 2019, https://www.investopedia.com/terms/p/peterlynch.asp.

84   "Wall $treet Week with Louis Rukeyser," *American Archive of Public Broadcasting* online, accessed October 17, 2022, https://americanarchive.org/special_collections/wall-street-week.

85   "C.G. Jung: Quotes," *Goodreads* online, accessed October 17, 2022, https://www.goodreads.com/quotes/290581-a-man-who-has-not-passed-through-the-inferno-of.

86   Farfromover403.eth, "Patterns Repeat, Because Human Nature Hasn't Changed for Thousands of Years," *Sundai Fungi Newsletter* online, accessed October 17, 2022, https://sundaifungi.substack.com/p/patterns-repeat-because-human-nature.

87   "Lao Tzu Quotes," *Goodreads* online, accessed October 17, 2022, https://www.goodreads.com/quotes/23420-be-careful-what-you-water-your-dreams-with-water-them.

88   Wilford Kale, "Tourist visits to state sites up 0.1% IN '90—blue ridge highlands region has biggest gain, 6.1 percent," *Richmond Times-Dispatch,* January 20, 1991.

89   Alan Watts, *Become What You Are* (Boston: Shambhala Publications, 2003), 29

90   Vernon Howard, *The Mystic Path to Cosmic Power* (New York: Parker Publishing, 1967), 112.

91   "National Asset Management Group," accessed October 17, 2022, https://www.namg.com/index.htm

92   "The Beverly Hillbillies," *Rotten Tomatoes* online, accessed October 17, 2022, https://www.rottentomatoes.com/m/1046435-beverly_hillbillies.

93   "The Beverly Hillbillies," *Britannica* **online**, August 31, 2022, https://www.britannica.com/topic/The-Beverly-Hillbillies.

94   *Deliverance*, IMDb online, accessed October 17, 2022, https://www.imdb.com/title/tt0068473/?ref_=nm_flmg_act_143.

95   *Scent of a Woman*, IMDb online, accessed October 17, 2022, https://www.imdb.com/title/tt0105323/?ref_=nv_sr_srsg_0.

96   "Dale Carnegie," *Britannica* **online, November 20, 2021, https://www.britannica.com/biography/Dale-Carnegie/additional-info#history.**

97   Sharon Penn, "Rules for Playing Best Ball Golf," Purdue University, accessed October 17, 2022, https://owl.purdue.edu/owl/research_and_citation/chicago_manual_17th_edition/cmos_formatting_and_style_guide/web_sources.html.

98   "Riverfront Stadium," *Ballparks by Munsey & Suppes* online, accessed October 17, 2022, https://ballparks.com/baseball/index.htm.

99   Craig Murder, "Bench's Homer Helps Push Reds into 1972 World Series," National Baseball Hall of Fame, accessed October 17, 2022, https://baseballhall.org/discover/inside-pitch/benchs-homer-propels-reds-to-1972-world-series.

100   "61+ Jesse Livermore Quotes About Money, Stocks and Success," *Kidadl* online, last modified October 3, 2022, https://kidadl.com/quotes/jesse-livermore-quotes-about-money-stocks-and-success.

101   Vincent van Gogh, "Letter to Theo, July 14 or 15, 1889," *Van Gogh Museum* online, accessed October 17, 2020, https://www.vangoghletters.org/vg/letters/let790/letter.html#translation.

102   "James Allen: Quotes," *Goodreads* online, accessed October 17, 2022, https://www.goodreads.com/quotes/92409-dream-lofty-dreams-and-as-you-dream-so-shall-you.

103   "Paul Stewart," Paul Stewart website, accessed October 17, 2022, https://www.paulstuart.com/mens/tailored-clothing/suits-and-tuxedos/?gclid=Cj0KCQjwhY-aBhCUARIsALNIC06vwmSJlmuQ--vXamL88dpzLCUiyY_sdQx46DkWlU2Xb8ktEklgILAaArszEALw_wcB.

104   "If you want to lift yourself up…," *Teach Different* online, accessed October 17, 2022, https://teachdifferent.com/podcast/if-you-want-to-lift-yourself-up-lift-up-someone-else-teach-different-with-booker-t-washington-self-development/

105   Andrew Whitby, "Who First Said…," last modified December 25, 2020, https://
        andrewwhitby.com/2020/12/25/if-you-want-to-go-fast/.

106   Hutt Bush, "Those Who Learned to Collaborate…" Being Point, accessed October
        17, 2022, https://beingpoint.com/those-who-learned-to-collaborate-and-improvise-
        most-effectively-have-prevailed-charles-darwin/.

107   "In basketball—as in life—true joy comes…," *Quotefancy* online, accessed October
        17, 2022, https://quotefancy.com/quote/1253454/Phil-Jackson-In-basketball-as-in-
        life-true-joy-comes-from-being-fully-present-in-each-and.

108   Larry Swedroe, "The Smartest Things Ever Said About Market Timing," CBS News
        online, updated on December 28, 2009. https://www.cbsnews.com/news/the-
        smartest-things-ever-said-about-market-timing/

109   *Seinfeld: The Opposite*, IMDb online, accessed October 17, 2022, https://www.imdb.
        com/title/tt0697744/.

110   "S&P 500 Total Returns," *Slickcharts* online, last modified October 18, 2022, https://
        www.slickcharts.com/sp500/returns.; "S&P 500: $100 in 1995…," accessed October
        18, 2022, https://www.officialdata.org/us/stocks/s-p-500/1995.

111   "NASDAQ Composite – 45 Year Historical Chart," Macrotrends, accessed October
        18, 2022, https://www.macrotrends.net/1320/nasdaq-historical-chart.; "1999
        NASDAQ 100 Historical Prices / Charts," FUTURES TradingCharts.com, accessed
        October 18, 2022, https://futures.tradingcharts.com/historical/ND/1999/0/
        continuous.html

112   Harry Guinness, "Apple Didn't Start in a Garage – What About Google, HP and
        Amazon?", MUO, last modified January 9, 2015, https://www.makeuseof.com/tag/
        apple-didnt-start-garage-google-hp-amazon/.; Chris Matyszczyk, "Woz: No, Apple
        Was Not Started in a Garage," CNET, last modified December 4, 2014, https://
        www.cnet.com/culture/woz-no-apple-was-not-started-in-a-garage/.; Alejandro Alba,
        "Steve Wozniak, Apple's Co-founder, Reveals that Apple Did Not Start in Garage,"
        last modified December 7, 2014, https://www.nydailynews.com/news/national/
        steve-wozniak-reveals-apple-not-start-garage-article-1.2037003.; Mary Meisenzahl,
        "Starting in a Garage Is Crucial…," Insider, last modified on April 1, 2020, https://
        www.businessinsider.com/google-apple-hp-microsoft-amazon-started-in-garages-
        photos-2019-12.

113   James A. Dorn, "Reflections on Greenspan's 'Irrational Exuberance' Speech after 25
        Years," CATO Institute, last modified on December 27, 2021, https://www.cato.org/
        blog/reflections-greenspans-irrational-exuberance-speech-after-25-years.

114   Adam Hayes, "Dotcom Bubble," last modified June 25, 2019, Investopedia, https://
        www.investopedia.com/terms/d/dotcom-bubble.asp.

115   Adam Hayes, "Irrational Exuberance," Investopedia, last modified April 8, 2022,
        https://www.investopedia.com/terms/i/irrationalexuberance.asp.

116	Maya Angelou, "It is time for parents to teach young people…" *Brainy Quote* online, accessed October 18, 2022, https://www.brainyquote.com/quotes/maya_angelou_132707.

117	Charles de Gaulle, "How can you govern a country…," *Britannica* **online, accessed October 18, 2022,** https://www.britannica.com/quotes/Charles-de-Gaulle-president-of-France.

118	Sun Tzu, "The Annotated Art of War," *Changing Minds* online, accessed October 18, 2022, http://changingminds.org/disciplines/warfare/art_war/sun_tzu_5-3.htm.

119	"A.A. Milne: Quotes," *Goodreads* online, accessed October 18, 2022, https://www.goodreads.com/quotes/70457-good-morning-eeyore-said-pooh-good-morning-pooh-bear-said.

120	*The Legend of Bagger Vance*, IMDb online, accessed October 18, 2022, https://www.imdb.com/title/tt0146984/?ref_=nv_sr_srsg_0.

121	*Extremely Loud and Incredibly Close*, IMDb online, accessed October 18, 2022, https://www.imdb.com/title/tt0477302/?ref_=nv_sr_srsg_0.

122	*Worth*, IMDb online, accessed October 18, 2022, https://www.imdb.com/title/tt8009744/?ref_=nv_sr_srsg_0.

123	Angela Ruth, "Paul Samuelson – Investing Is Like Watching Grass Grow," Due, last modified June 13, 2022, https://due.com/blog/paul-samuelson-investing-is-like-watching-grass-grow/.

124	"If you can't sleep at night…," *Quotefancy* online, accessed October 18, 2022, https://quotefancy.com/quote/1639507/Jesse-Lauriston-Livermore-If-you-can-t-sleep-at-night-because-of-your-stock-market.

125	John P. Reese, "Winning in the Market with the Patience of the Wright Brothers and Warren Buffet," Forbes, last modified January 30, 2018, https://www.forbes.com/sites/investor/2018/01/30/winning-in-the-market-with-the-patience-of-the-wright-brothers-and-warren-buffett/?sh=3b159236633b.

126	The Pine Club website, accessed October 18, 2022, https://thepineclub.com/.

127	Amelia Robinson, "Dayton Woman Ate at the Pine Club with her Aunt Barbara and Uncle George," last modified December 4, 2018, https://www.daytondailynews.com/news/local/dayton-woman-ate-pine-club-with-her-aunt-barbara-and-uncle-george/pnj2yPFD57gRasqu8xB8aO/; Lisa Powell, "Pine Club History…," last modified on February 28, 2019, https://www.journal-news.com/news/local/pine-club-history-quirky-facts-about-dayton-iconic-steakhouse/LOLrc7OVZd2LrNvaN0FjAP/; Lauren Durham, "The Pine Club: A Steakhouse Built on Simplicity and Success," *Flyer News*, last modified November 30, 2019, https://flyernews.com/ae/the-pine-club-a-steakhouse-built-on-simplicity-and-success/11/30/2019/; Caleb Stephens, "Mystique, Great Steaks Makes Pine Club Special Place," *Dayton Business Journal* online, last modified March 10, 2008, https://www.bizjournals.com/dayton/stories/2008/03/10/tidbits2.html.

128   "The History of Baldwin Pianos," *Living Pianos* online, accessed October 18, 2022, https://livingpianos.com/the-history-of-baldwin-pianos/.

129   "Baldwin Piano & Organ Company…," *Reference for Business* online, accessed October 18, 2022, https://www.referenceforbusiness.com/history2/67/Baldwin-Piano-Organ-Company.html.

130   "Baldwin Piano Company Company [sic] History Timeline," *Zippia* online, accessed October 18, 2022, https://www.zippia.com/baldwin-piano-organ-company-careers-16115/history/

131   "Baldwin Piano & Organ Company History," *Funding Universe* online, accessed October 18, 2022, http://www.fundinguniverse.com/company-histories/baldwin-piano-organ-company-history/.

132   "Baldwin Piano & Organ Company…," *Reference for Business* online, accessed October 18, 2022, https://www.referenceforbusiness.com/history2/67/Baldwin-Piano-Organ-Company.html.

133   "Sour Notes: How Baldwin-United Expanded from Pianos to Trouble," from *Hearings Before a Subcommittee of the Committee on Government Operations House of Representatives Ninety-Eighth Congress*, p.627, March 15 and 16, 1983, https://books.google.com/books?id=GZKqWbZPQzU C&pg=PA627&lpg=PA627&dq=baldwin+pianos+and+sperry+and+hutc hinson&source=bl&ots=IKMPF-Sd-4&sig=ACfU3U28Ibz9sduHjT23_ J0_hubXNDXLzw&hl=en&sa=X&ved=2ahUKEwiP_ tmsndn6AhUDoFsKHdreAMYQ6AF6BAhdEAM#v=onepage&q=baldwin%20 pianos%20and%20sperry%20and%20hutchinson&f=false.

134   "MGIC Investment Corp. Would Become a Subsidiary of Baldwin-United," *UPI* online, last modified December 15, 1981, https://www.upi.com/ Archives/1981/12/15/MGIC-Investment-Corp-would-become-a-subsidiary-of-Baldwin-United/5205377240400/.

135   "Morley Thompson Obituary," *Legacy* online, accessed October 18, 2022, https://www.legacy.com/us/obituaries/cincinnati/name/morley-thompson-obituary?id=22898497.

136   "MGIC Investment Corp. – Company Profile…," *Reference for Business* online, accessed October 18, 2022, https://www.referenceforbusiness.com/history2/46/MGIC-Investment-Corp.html.

137   Ibid.

138   "James Chanos," *Yale School of Management* online, accessed October 18, 2022, https://som.yale.edu/faculty/james-chanos.

139   "Jim Chanos Masterclass," Intelligent Investor, accessed October 18, 2022, https://ii-uploads.s3.amazonaws.com/share_advisor/splreports/II_SR_Jim_Chanos_Masterclass__Dec_14.pdf.

140   "Baldwin Piano & Organ Company History," *Funding Universe* online, accessed October 18, 2022, http://www.fundinguniverse.com/company-histories/baldwin-piano-organ-company-history/.

141   "Baldwin Piano & Organ Company – Company Profile…," *Reference for Business* online, "Decrescendo" subhead, accessed October 18, 2022, https://www.referenceforbusiness.com/history2/67/Baldwin-Piano-Organ-Company.html.

142   Michael Blumstein, "Baldwin, a Casualty of Fast Expansion, Files for Bankruptcy," *The New York Times*, last modified September 27, 1983, https://www.nytimes.com/1983/09/27/business/baldwin-a-casualty-of-fast-expansion-files-for-bankruptcy.html?pagewanted=all.

143   "Houston Pipe Line Co LP," *Bloomberg* online, accessed October 18, 2022, https://www.bloomberg.com/profile/company/0743448D:US?leadSource=uverify%20wall.

144   Michael Frontain, "Lay, Kenneth Lee," last modified May 3, 2017, https://www.tshaonline.org/handbook/entries/lay-kenneth-lee.

145   Troy Segal, "Enron Scandal: The Fall of a Wall Street Darling," Investopedia, last modified November 26, 2021, https://www.investopedia.com/updates/enron-scandal-summary/.

146   Peter Bondarenko, "Enron Scandal," last modified August 13, 2022, *Britannica* online, https://www.britannica.com/event/Enron-scandal.

147   Adam Hayes, "Bernie Madoff: Who He Was, How His Ponzi Scheme Worked," Investopedia, last updated September 8, 2022, https://www.investopedia.com/terms/b/bernard-madoff.asp.

148   Keyede Erinfolami, "The 9 Biggest Risks for Crypto Investors (Both Beginners and Veterans," Muo, last modified November 28, 2021, https://www.makeuseof.com/biggest-risks-crypto-investors/.

149   "Edwin Lefèvre: Quotes," accessed October 18, 2022, https://www.goodreads.com/quotes/9024176-another-lesson-i-learned-early-is-that-there-is-nothing.

150   Nick Maggiulli, "The Greatest Investment Quotes of All Time," Of Dollars and Data, last modified March 26, 2020, https://ofdollarsanddata.com/investment-quotes/.

151   Tobias Weaver, "Carl Jung Greatest Quotes," Orion, last modified July 18, 2022, https://www.orionphilosophy.com/stoic-blog/carl-jung-greatest-quotes.

152   *Step into Liquid*, IMDb online, accessed October 18, 2022, https://www.imdb.com/title/tt0308508/.

153   *Blue Hawaii*, IMDb online, accessed October 18, 2022, https://www.imdb.com/title/tt0054692/?ref_=nv_sr_srsg_0.

154   "Davy surfing in Hawaii in late 1966 (photo)," *Monkees Live Almanac* (blog), January 20, 2017, https://www.monkeeslivealmanac.com/blog/davy-surfing-in-hawaii-in-late-1966.

155 Manoj Singh, "The 2007-2008 Financial Crisis in Review," Investopedia, last modified September 18, 2022, https://www.investopedia.com/articles/economics/09/financial-crisis-review.asp.

156 Chris Isidore, "Bailout Plan Rejected – Supporters Scramble," CNN Money, last modified September 29, 2008, https://money.cnn.com/2008/09/29/news/economy/bailout/.

157 Kimberly Amadeo, "The Stock Market Crash of 2008," The Balance, last modified May 25, 2022, https://www.thebalancemoney.com/stock-market-crash-of-2008-3305535.

158 John Weinberg, "The Great Recession and Its Aftermath," Federal Reserve History, last modified November 22, 2013, https://www.federalreservehistory.org/essays/great-recession-and-its-aftermath.

159 "Victory at Sea," *Urban Dictionary* online, accessed October 18, 2022, https://www.urbandictionary.com/define.php?term=Victory%20at%20sea.

160 Michael J. Boyle, "What Is the History of the S&P 500 Stock Index?", last modified October 5, 2022, https://www.investopedia.com/ask/answers/041015/what-history-sp-500.asp; Kimberly Amadeo, "The Stock Market Crash of 2008," The Balance, last modified May 25, 2022, https://www.thebalancemoney.com/stock-market-crash-of-2008-3305535.; *Yahoo Finance* online, accessed October 18, 2022, https://shorturl.at/jDJN8

161 Reem Heakal, "What Is The Glass–Steagall Act of 1933? Purpose and Effect," Investopedia, last modified September 25, 2022, https://www.investopedia.com/articles/03/071603.asp.

162 John V. Duca, "Subprime Mortgage Crisis," Federal Reserve History, last modified November 22, 2013, https://www.federalreservehistory.org/essays/subprime-mortgage-crisis.

163 Nirvikar Singh, "The Ostrich and Dr. Doom," Mint, last modified September 22, 2008, https://www.livemint.com/Opinion/1VeKWOkGxBrJF1O1qQk1WK/The-Ostrich-and-Dr-Doom.html.

164 *The Big Short*, IMDb online, accessed October 18, 2022, https://www.imdb.com/title/tt1596363/?ref_=fn_tt_tt_1.

165 The Rolling Stones, "You Can't Always Get What You Want," (Official Lyric Video), https://www.youtube.com/watch?v=krxU5Y9lCS8.

166 C. Ledger, "Alan Watts, Muddy Water, and Meditating," Medium, last modified July 25, 2015, https://medium.com/meditation-without-mysticism/alan-watts-muddy-water-and-meditating-49a8211cff8d.

167 Benjamin Graham, The Intelligent Investor- Revised Edition, (New York: HarperBusiness, 2006).

168   "Wide Area Telephone Service (WATS)," *Technopedia* online, accessed October 18, 2022, https://www.techopedia.com/definition/9998/wide-area-telephone-service-wats.

169   "Batphone," *Batman Fandom* online, accessed October 18, 2022, https://batman.fandom.com/wiki/Batphone.

170   "Ken Griffey," *Baseball Reference* online, accessed October 18, 2022, https://www.baseball-reference.com/players/g/griffke01.shtml.